The Whole Career Sourcebook

Robbie Miller Kaplan

amacom

American Management Association

This book is available at a special
discount when ordered in bulk quantities.
For information, contact Special Sales Department,
AMACOM, a division of American Management Association,
135 West 50th Street, New York, NY 10020.

This publication is designed to provide accurate and authorita-
tive information in regard to the subject matter covered. It is
sold with the understanding that the publisher is not engaged in
rendering legal, accounting, or other professional service. If legal
advice or other expert assistance is required, the services of a
competent professional person should be sought.

Library of Congress Cataloging-in-Publication Data

Kaplan, Robbie Miller.
    The whole career sourcebook / Robbie Miller Kaplan.
        p.   cm.
    Includes index.
    ISBN 0-8144-7752-6
    1. Career changes. I. Title.
  HF5384.K37 1991
  650.14—dc20   91-16701
                                              CIP

Printing number

10 9 8 7 6 5 4 3 2 1

To the
special women
in my life:

My daughters,
Sam and Julie

My sisters,
Judy and Margie

Contents

Preface

I have written *The Whole Career Sourcebook* for *two* types of people: those who have a job and those who don't. Why have I written it? Because just as the companies most of us work for are changing the way they do business in order to compete in the global *marketplace*, so do all of us have to take control of our careers in order to compete in the global *workplace.*

I am a strong believer in career development, in paying close and constant attention to career efforts and direction. Work is just too important to let those who do not have your best interests at heart make decisions for you. Reading and using *The Whole Career Sourcebook* will help you assume control of your career and identify work experiences that are satisfying and fulfilling.

This combination how-to-book and directory holds a lot of information between its covers. You will find a clearly worked out career planning process, as well as advice on job-hunting techniques, effective interviewing skills, and résumé and cover-letter writing ideas. And you will learn how to look for business, industry, and career trends, as well as how to research organizations and salaries.

What career opportunities are available for the 1990s? As a result of my research and conversations with labor market and human resources experts, I have uncovered the eight skills being cited as the most desirable and the four career areas that are providing the greatest opportunities for employment through the end of this decade.

There are literally thousands of resources available that address different aspects of career development. To help you separate the wheat from the chaff, I have reviewed over 300 of the best career resources available. You'll find detailed information on hundreds of books, workbooks, booklets, vocational inventories, newsletters, magazines, newspapers, computer software programs, audiotapes, and video programs. I am not endorsing these products or suggesting that you purchase them. They are here for you to consider. Each resource listing includes an address, phone number, and brief description.

During the process of writing and compiling *The Whole Career Sourcebook*, I met and spoke with many people. From career and industry experts to real-life career builders, they all willingly share their advice and experiences with you throughout these pages (some of their names have been changed to provide anonimity).

I hope you will use *The Whole Career Sourcebook* as your passport to career discovery. By uncovering your career options, you will be set for an adventure that will reward you for the rest of your working life.

Enjoy the trip.

                                                    Robbie Miller Kaplan

Acknowledgments

A special thank-you to:

My husband, Jim Kaplan, who graciously provided assistance, support, and encouragement
My editor, Andrea Pedolsky, a pleasure to work with, for providing her expertise and encouragement
Nancy Wallace, for her friendship, enthusiasm, suggestions, and review of the manuscript

Many thanks to the following people who willingly gave me their time and shared their expertise:

Jim Anderson, Judy Barclay, Jeanne Barnes, Bernadette Black, Angie Carrera, Bruce Crockett of Comsat Corporation, Gail Crockett, John Crum of First City Capital Corporation, Mary Fairchild, Mark Griffin, Barry Hatfield, Stan Paul, Ken Plum, Senta Raizen of National Center for Improving Science Education, Wade Robinson of UNISYS Corporation, Karen Romano-Taylor, John Rupple, Judy Sansbury, Nancy Schuman of Career Blazers Personnel Services, Dorothy Shean, Rich Stacy of INOVA Health Systems, Mike Townshend of New Options Group, Inc., Judy Vance, Brenda Watson of *The New York Times*, and Francine Zucker.

I gratefully acknowledge the following books on quotations:

The Speaker's Book of Quotations by Henry O. Dormann (New York: Fawcett, 1987)
The Manager's Book of Quotations by Lewis D. Eigen and Jonathan P. Siegel (New York: AMACOM Books, 1989)

Chapter 1

Career Building

Everything's changed. Leveraged buyouts, joint ventures, divestitures, mergers, acquisitions, restructuring, and takeovers (hostile or otherwise) have altered the workplace and changed the personality, structure, goals, makeup, and sometimes even the very existence of the organizations you came to know and trust.

> Change is the law of the future. And those who look only to the past or present are certain to miss the future.
>
> John Fitzgerald Kennedy

Do you remember Burroughs Corporation? It bought Sperry Corporation in 1986, but it's no longer called Burroughs *or* Sperry; it's now UNISYS Corporation. Sometimes the name is the only thing that doesn't change. Take Garfinckel's Department Store, for example. It was acquired by Allied Stores Corporation in 1981, which was acquired by the Campeau Corporation in 1986. The Campeau Corporation sold Garfinckel's to Raleigh Stores Corporation in 1987, and Garfinckel's, unable to survive the shifts in ownership and direction, filed for bankruptcy in 1990.

We've added the word *downsizing* to our vocabulary, which refers to the practice of streamlining an organization and making it more profitable by eliminating positions and saving money. It's an interesting process, unless you happen to hold the position that's being eliminated.

Can you remember when people studied and prepared for occupations and worked in the same job and organization until retirement? Loyalty in the workplace has not only decreased, it's ceasing to exist.

1

Employees no longer consider organizational tenure a priority; often they change jobs and careers five times or more during their lifetimes. On their part, employers are laying off tenured staff or offering them early retirement.

You can't take job security for granted anymore either. Federal, state, and local governments, always secure work havens, have recently experienced budget deficits and funding cuts and have instituted hiring freezes and, in some cases, layoffs.

But you've changed too. Do you still have the same values, interests, and needs? Perhaps you've performed the same job and work activities for three, five, or ten years and want or need more challenge, something new or different.

What are your options? The goal of employment with the same organization for your entire work life, complete with retirement and a gold watch, is no longer a reality. So, if ever there was a time for you to take control of your career, it's now.

No one is watching out for you and nurturing your career. No one is plotting your career growth and progress and planning your next promotion. No one is guiding or encouraging you to develop skills that will keep pace with technological changes and advances.

But the good news is, You are in charge of your career. It's time to take control and aim in the directions that *you* desire, and that *you* plan. Get ready to control your career destiny, and start planning now to reap the satisfaction and benefits of working and loving it, of growing and developing new skills, and of experiencing and meeting the challenges of tomorrow.

While you may not know exactly what tomorrow holds for you, one thing is certain. Tomorrow will be different. You can't hide from the inevitable changes, and you're better off directing and controlling your future to meet them.

It's scary to take the controls when you've never been the pilot. But what if your organization begins downsizing or the rumor of a merger becomes a reality? Would you make plans and prepare and anticipate change, or would you deal with a potential layoff by climbing into bed and pulling the covers over your head? Scarlett O'Hara may "think about it tomorrow," but you're better off thinking about it today.

When Xerox Corporation faced tough competition with foreign imports, Stan Paul saw the change in his organization as it began to lose its competitive edge in the marketplace. He decided it was time to change jobs and break into a different industry.

> I decided in 1980, after a successful career with Xerox, that I needed to make a change. Anticipating the move, I took a sales position within Xerox to gain marketing experience. I

felt the computer industry was hot and decided to change industries. It wasn't a smooth transition.

When you work for a large corporation, you are controlled, and that's a big problem because it almost plans your career for you. I had no experience planning my career, and I made this major transition without adequate planning.

I experienced setbacks—had to pay my dues again—but persevered and eventually came out ahead. In retrospect, I should have had a road map, been more patient in making the transition, and spent some time in a related field. I learned that I had to package myself and write a résumé that highlighted the appropriate experiences and skills. In my case, I needed a totally different approach, moving from a large corporation to a small one, as well as changing industries. It took me several years in the new industry to learn a successful approach.

I took my previous experience for granted and have learned a lot about myself. I have a knack for cleaning up operations and putting them back together. I sell myself on my successes; employers are looking for you to tie together your skills and accomplishments.

I encourage others to plan and make transitions. Nowadays, any company is up for sale. People should take a good look at their careers in their company and industry. If you're thinking of making a transition, get out and talk to people and find out the skills you'll need. If possible, reposition yourself in your company to acquire needed skills. Stay current by reading industry and business literature. It's important to build a network that'll support you in your transition.

In this dynamic business environment, you must prepare yourself for change. If your company is bought out and you don't have a job, you'll lack confidence and lose self-esteem. Most people don't flourish on uncertainty. Beware of stepping into something that is not a good match. While rejection is tough, successful people take the time to evaluate themselves and their options before jumping into a new situation.

What are your options? Your possibilities are limited only by your imagination and drive. You can change jobs, industries, or careers or combine options, such as staying in the same career but looking for a job in a different industry. Or, you can change careers within your company and change jobs or industries in the future, or leave your organization and start your own business. But whatever you choose to do, don't scrap your history; rather, build on your skills, experience, and accomplishments.

Barry Hatfield did just that. He began working for AT&T in marketing and chose other jobs and experiences within AT&T to build additional skills. When divestiture hit, AT&T experienced downsizing and Barry made plans to fulfill a dream of starting his own business.

> AT&T staffed up heavily during divestiture, to meet an initial increased work load, and then literally discarded people. They laid off thousands of people who had given twenty to twenty-five years of service to the company.
>
> It became apparent that the opportunities for advancement within AT&T were limited. As opposed to upward, I set my sights on outward and moved into areas where I would have the opportunity to develop new skills and bring my expertise to other departments. I focused on developing the financial knowledge I needed and was afforded some wonderful jobs within AT&T. These positions provided the economic expertise needed to facilitate my own service business.
>
> The limited upward mobility and upper management's fear of layoffs caused most executives to take the no-risk position of "no decision is the only safe decision." This stagnation period told me that now was the time to move on. The key element in reaching this conclusion was that I wanted to be able to control my own destiny, but I still had not finalized all the aspects of the company I dreamed of building. Spending many hours planning at home, I took a job with another firm in a similar business [to the one he later set up] to enhance my knowledge base. After one and a half years, I was prepared to execute my business plan.
>
> With a formalized and detailed business plan, I spent six months satisfying registration and licensing requirements and preparing for the business opening. Initially, I ran it all myself and discovered two valuable lessons: First, before you make your first transaction, find a good attorney, one who really understands what you're doing. Second, set up a realistic business plan and then immediately look for bank financing.
>
> My company is now two-and-a-half years old. I've found a niche in the communications and computer industry, as evidenced by a growth rate of 33 to 40 percent per

year. I realize that starting my own business was a high risk; a gamble that is resulting in high rewards. I'm no longer constrained by management indecision and my destiny is only limited by my own efforts and ingenuity. It's certainly the most satisfying thing I've done and I'm happier now than I've ever been.

I believe entrepreneurship opportunities are unlimited. I encourage anyone who has the dream to act on it. You have to have initiative, be a self-starter, and have thick skin to endure rejection. As long as you work for someone else, you are building their net worth and not necessarily doing a whole lot for your own bottom line. If you want to be challenged daily for the next ten years, struggle, fight and claw for survival, then how can you pass up the opportunity of owning your own business?

There's an old saying, "A change is as good as a rest." I'm sure that whoever came up with that expression never went through a restructuring where their job or entire department was eliminated.

Carolyn M., a recent job hunter, worked for five and a half years in a job that was a blend of everything she loved: marketing, traveling, and educating, and she developed a special niche in introducing software systems to financial institutions.

The financial services industry, once booming, hit a major slump and Carolyn's department and her position were eliminated.

If you are let go, you have some basic decisions to make. Are you going to stay in the same industry? The same job family? Do you want to work for a large company? Small company? Do you want to work independently, be a team member, or a manager? You've got an opportunity to make a positive change in your life and it is up to you to make the change a positive one.

Getting a job is a job. Basically, you've got a lot of studying and thinking to do about jobs and companies you find most attractive, so you should start your approach there.

Wade Robinson,
Director, Planning and Staffing,
UNISYS Defense Systems

I had developed a specialty, and when my position was eliminated, I didn't see a fit anywhere else in the company. I could have worked within the system, but decided I was ready for a change.

I took a severance package, and for close to six months, I worked every day looking for a job. My job search was carefully planned. I defined what I enjoyed about my last job, which was the majority of my work, and my first step was to talk with people in financial institutions with marketing departments. After meeting with approximately fifty individuals, the news wasn't encouraging. Organizations that had never experienced layoffs were now laying off people. Realizing this field wasn't going to work, I then pursued my other specialty, information systems.

My job search strategy consisted of answering classified ads in newspapers, newsletters, and leads from associations, direct mail marketing, as well as networking. I targeted myself to make ten phone calls a day, but gave myself flexibility in balancing meetings and calls. There were days that I made ten to fourteen calls and others when I couldn't pick up the phone. When that happened, I used my time to read articles, books, and periodicals.

Initially, I used a script when making calls. Very briefly, in two minutes, I wanted to get across that I was in the job market, that so and so had recommended that I call, that I wanted to come and meet with this person and get their views on the work place. The individual might ask for more information about the type of job or industry and what I was looking for and I would tell them. I always ended the conversation by requesting the names of other people I could talk to. My goal was to get two names from every call. I sometimes got ten or twelve names; other times, none. I didn't push or irritate people, just thanked them for their time and moved on.

I went on job interviews, wrote thank-you notes, made follow-up phone calls, and sent replies to newspaper clippings. I eventually got a lead from a colleague I had worked with ten years ago. I pursued it, was offered and accepted the position. My new job is similiar to my previous one, but in a different industry.

I tell other job seekers, it's a job looking for a job! You can't be shy and meek because there's too much competition. Don't take rejection personally. It took me much longer than I had anticipated to find another job. Look for support from your friends and family and constantly keep your goals in mind.

If you want to find the exact niche, you can. You become very intuitive when you go into offices and meet with people. You quickly pick up the culture and whether you would work well in this environment. I recommend using your antennae and your senses.

This experience has taught me to handle my career differently. I really enjoyed what I was doing and wanted to be there forever. I didn't want to face the reality of change and now, no matter how much I enjoy a position, I will still think of change and how change can be placed on you whether or not you want to change. I'll keep my résumé updated and I'll build more of a network. I'll plan to always be a member of at least one professional association.

Remember, it's a numbers game and the more people you contact, the greater your chances of success. It requires persistence and hard work but it's worth it when you find the job that's right for you.

Whatever your current work situation, happy or unhappy, secure or insecure, it's time for you to make some plans. Without a crystal ball, no one can foresee all the changes in store, but if you're directing your career, you can successfully navigate your future. That's what career building is all about: planning your career by building on your strengths, skills, abilities, and accomplishments. You don't begin again, scrapping your work history, training, and education, you make changes that utilize your experiences and talents.

Career building begins by understanding yourself: your likes, dislikes, skills, abilities, interests, and values. What appeals to you and what would you enjoy doing? What careers, position, and fields give you pleasure and offer challenge and growth? A firm foundation enables you to make career and job decisions that are in tune with what would make you happy. You must understand yourself to provide a foundation for making your career decisions. If you don't, you'll never be able to choose work experiences, industries, or directions that are satisfying. It's like getting in a car and moving out in traffic with no map, no direction, unsure where you're going, how long it will take, and whether you'll even know when you've arrived. Getting to know yourself helps to minimize career risks, because you'll be more certain of the outcome.

Once you've built the foundation, continue to be aware of what's happening around you, in your career, the workplace, the business world, and the world in general. Once you know yourself, validate that your plans and career desires are realistic. Read, discover, and follow business trends and news and adapt your career plans as needed. Keeping current throughout your career will help to increase your options and keep you positioned in areas of growth.

You'll need numerous materials and resources for your career building. You'll find that connecting with other people is your best source of information, resources, and job opportunities. Making connections is a vital link to the future, providing the tools and support for your career success and satisfaction.

Even after you've identified your existing skills, your learning isn't over. Career building requires a commitment to lifelong learning. As changes occur, you will adapt and develop skills to meet current and future work requirements and needs. By developing an expertise in skills that employers find desirable, you can successfully compete in the workplace. Part of this development process involves discovering and identifying what skills you'll need; the other involves acquiring the skills and preparing yourself for the future. You'll continue to learn and develop new skills for the rest of your working life.

Another brick in building a career is learning and utilizing effective job hunting techniques. You'll be selling yourself to employers by marketing your skills, experience, and contributions with a résumé or an application. Get ahead of the competition for job opportunities by uncovering new sources for job leads and plan a strategy to find opportunities, interview effectively, and win the job of your choice.

It's all here, in this book process by process, level by level, chapter by chapter. It's not easy, but it's not only possible, it's achievable. Careers don't just happen, they're built, and the effort you put into career building will result in career progression, continuation, and satisfaction. If you do meet unexpected career and employment changes, anywhere along the way, you'll be prepared to pursue alternative plans and successfully work through the change.

Chapter 2

Know Thyself

The key to career satisfaction is knowing what kind of work and activities give you pleasure. If you base a career on employment trends alone, without considering your own interests and skills, you may wind up hating it. And you'll never enjoy your work or rise to the top doing something you dislike, because your dissatisfaction will show. But if you build your career on what you really like and want to do, use the skills and abilities that you want to use, and have work experiences that make you feel good about yourself, your pleasure will be visible in everything you do.

Knowing yourself is the key that unlocks the door to a satisfying career. The journey of self-exploration, discovery, and understanding described here is a process that examines your past, identifies your strengths and interests, and enables you to plan for the future. Individuals move through this process at their own pace. Some prepare for the future while others wait until they're burned or forced out. Pain can be an effective motivator. You alone will know when it is time for you to embark on this journey.

Career planning is a process that unleashes the power within us to create the future we want. If we choose not to invest the time and effort into designing our own future, we may never experience the joy and fulfillment that meaningful work can provide.

Nancy Wallace,
Assistant Director, Career Planning Services,
George Mason University

Be prepared to commit yourself to the process. It takes time and discipline and requires a great deal of introspection, but the effort will pay off. The more you learn about yourself, the easier it is to make satisfying choices and decisions.

You'll base your career choices on the following elements: interests, likes, dislikes, skills, abilities, and values. You're not the same person you were ten years ago, nor are you the person you will be three years from now. Self-discovery is an ongoing process. As your experiences, values, and interests change, so will your career choices. Arrange a periodic career assessment, just as you would schedule a checkup for your car. Consider it career maintenance to encourage growth and prevent yourself from career frustration.

The best decisions are those made with research and information. A thorough self-analysis enables you to make informed career decisions and prepares you for career change and opportunity.

The Elements of Planning Your Career

When you bake a cake, you use a plan to guide you, called a recipe. The recipe tells you what ingredients and amounts to use and how long to mix and bake. If you experiment, shortcut the process, or disregard the recipe, the cake may still be okay but, more likely, it will flop. Your chances of producing a successful outcome are greater if you follow the recipe.

The recipe for a successful career is career planning, and the first step is defining the elements of the career planning process: interests, skills, abilities, likes, dislikes, and values.

Interests

Your interests are preferences for activities that you alone choose to pursue. At some time or other, we all engage in activities selected for us. While some of these activities may be appealing, chances are they reflect someone else's interests.

You have to like what you do in order to enjoy your work. Work that is chosen based on your interests increases the odds for work satisfaction. You won't need to hire a detective to uncover your interests. Look for clues in activities that give you pleasure, your past and present interests, and ask yourself these questions:

- What do you do for fun?
- What hobbies, books, and subjects do you or would you choose to explore?

- What did you dream of doing when you grew up?
- What do you dream of doing now?
- What experiences would you like to try?

Skills

A skill is the ability to effectively perform an activity. You are not born with skills; rather they are developed and learned; expertise is gained by studying and practicing. Identifying, adding, and polishing your skills is an integral part of the career building process.

In *The Three Boxes of Life,** Richard Bolles identifies three categories of skills.

> Identify your skills by looking at your successes and what you really enjoy doing in life. Look back over your work and volunteer history and what you do in the family that gives you a real thrill. People need to build on the thrills they get, the skills and abilities that really make them feel good about themselves. Always build on what you really like to do. It is always a pleasure to learn something that you want to learn.
>
> Bernadette Black,
> Counselor and author of *Training for Life*

1. *Functional skills* relate to the basic elements of a task and fall under three groupings: skills with people, information or data, and things. These skills usually transfer easily from job to job. Examples include:

- Planning
- Supervising
- Researching
- Preparing budgets
- Making decisions
- Handling details
- Monitoring policies
- Implementing new systems
- Writing speeches

2. *Work content skills* are learned and used primarily to perform a job and include special vocabulary, specific knowledge, and technical

*Berkeley, Calif.: Ten Speed Press, 1981.

ability. These skills are usually acquired in formal settings such as colleges, universities, vocational and technical schools, continuing education, apprenticeship programs, and on-the-job or company training. Some examples include:

- Medical skills
  —Drawing blood
  —Taking X-rays
  —Compounding and dispensing medications
  —Cleaning and maintaining lab equipment
  —Administering first aid treatment
- Technical skills
  —Architectural drafting
  —Testing, adjusting, and repairing equipment
  —Building experimental equipment and models
  —Performing quality control testing
- Programming skills
  —Writing computer programs in UNIX

3. *Self-management skills* are personality traits that stay with us and which we bring from job to job. For example:

- Resourcefulness
- Dedication
- Persistence

It is important to identify not only your existing skills but those you will need to further and enhance your career. It may be hard for you to pinpoint your skills. People often take their skills for granted and ask, "Can't everyone do this?" Each individual has different skills and strengths. You are unique and need to identify your talents.

Abilities

Abilities are a natural potential and are very different from skills. You are born with abilities. You either have them or you don't. We all know of some individual with an ear for music who mastered a musical instrument in a few years. Maybe you struggled with violin lessons and finally gave up. We often say, "She took to swimming like a duck to water" or, "Math came so easily to him."

Abilities are natural gifts. You may want to pursue math, science, computers, writing, or art. There is a greater potential for success if you have a natural ability for the career or work experience you pursue.

Some people go through life never tapping into their abilities; others use them much later in life. A good example of what we sometimes call a late bloomer is Jim Weil. He wanted to take an electronics course after high school but was persuaded to go to college and get a degree in accounting instead. When personal computers were introduced, Jim found he had a natural ability to work with them. He has since become a personal computer expert within his organization and now writes a column on PC applications for an accounting journal.

Likes and Dislikes

The exciting part of the self-discovery process is discovering new things about yourself. You will probably find that you have many more skills than you had imagined and may even uncover aptitudes or interests that have been latent for years.

When you assess your interests, skills, and abilities, it is important to differentiate which ones you would like to use. You may have very desirable skills but if you dislike using them and they do not bring you pleasure, you would be wise to choose a work setting and career that will utilize other skills.

- What do you like about your job? Dislike?
- What did you like about past jobs? Dislike?

The probability of finding happiness in your career increases with using only the interests, skills, and abilities that you enjoy. For this reason, it is important to take your discoveries and determine what you like and dislike. Build on your likes and discard the dislikes. You will never find satisfaction doing what you don't like.

Values

Values are basic beliefs. Our most satisfying experiences are those that we choose based on our personal values. If you choose a career based on someone else's values, chances are you will not be happy.

Value is the worth that we place on our work. If work experiences are chosen based on your values, your work will have meaning and increase your self-esteem. It is hard to give your all to work that has no purpose or value.

Identify your values by looking at the past and to the future: What work experiences have you valued in the past and why? What are your dreams for the future? Values are not set in stone. As you move through life, as the decades change, and as you experience life and death, highs and lows, your values will change. Annually assess your values to ensure that you know what is important to you, and act on that knowledge.

Navigating the Career Planning Process

Now that you understand the elements of career planning, it is time to chart your individual course of self-discovery. How you proceed on this journey is up to you. There are numerous vocational inventories and instruments, books, workbooks, computer software programs, and workshops that can guide you through the process. You will probably need to try a combination of tools to identify all the pieces. Some individuals look to vocational inventories and instruments to supply the answers. While these can help identify skills and interests, they alone are not an answer. Inventories and instruments are most effective when they validate information that you have already discovered about yourself.

You have the choice of working independently, with a group, or one-on-one with a career counselor. Many different services are available at a wide range of cost. Look into what is offered and choose the services and products that work best for you. Choose a course of action that fits your learning style as well as your pocketbook. To help you work through the process, the following sections offer various resources, tools, and options that will assist you in finding the means to identify the points of information to help you chart your course.

Remember, it took a long time for you to grow to this point. It takes time to clarify information about yourself and learn your special interests, skills, abilities, and values—the uniqueness that is you. There is no quick fix, no one tool that will tell you what to do.

According to Sally R., Career and Management Consultant:

> I began my career in retailing. While I liked the work, I hated the hours and pay and lasted only a year and a half. I then found a job with Xerox Corporation in their customer service department and it was pure luck that the job matched my skills and interests. I spent the next eight years with Xerox and my career offered great challenge and growth. I had the opportunity to develop additional skills and take on new responsibilities. Unfortunately, I allowed the company to plan my career and I eventually burned out and quit.
>
> It was time for another career change. I knew that I had marketable skills but in a new position, I only wanted to use the skills that gave me pleasure and satisfaction. My goal was to love my work.

I went back to college for a year to complete my bachelor's degree. During this time, I did extensive self-analysis to determine my skills, interests, values, likes, and dislikes. *Wishcraft* by Barbara Sher helped me identify and target a career in training. I translated my management and personnel experiences at Xerox into creating and presenting workshops on how to find jobs.

The past eight years in my career have been very rewarding. I have continued to build my skills and experiences and my career now includes writing, training, and administering in the areas of career and management development. I have identified clear patterns of skills and accomplishments throughout my career. My strengths lie in oral and written communications and a love of working with people. I now know that this pattern will always be reflected in the work experiences I choose.

I took the Myer-Briggs Type Indicator (MBTI) through a professional development course and it gave me great insight into myself and my work environment. I wish that I had taken it earlier in my career as it would have helped direct and support my career goals. I have learned that the more you know about yourself, the easier it is to choose experiences that will bring you career and personal satisfaction.

Terms and References You Need to Know About

Holland's theory   John Holland, a career theoretician, developed a theory of vocational choice referred to as Holland's Theory or RIASEC Theory. The theory states that individuals will find greater career satisfaction if they choose occupational environments that are consistent with their interests and competencies. The occupational environments that he has identified, also referred to as the Holland Personality Types, are: realistic, investigative, artistic, social, enterprising, or conventional.

Jung's theory   Carl Jung, one of the world's renowned psychiatrists and a contemporary of Sigmund Freud's who developed the theory of psychological types. The theory refers to basic differences in the way individuals prefer to use their perception and judgment that result in differences in behavior. Perception involves the way individuals take in information and what they see in a situation, and judgment is the way they come to conclusions and what they decide to do about what they have perceived.

Dictionary of Occupational Titles (DOT)   Directory that identifies nearly 20,000 job titles and classifies jobs by the type of work done, required training, physical demands, and work conditions. Published by the U.S. Department of Labor.

Guide for Occupational Exploration (GOE)   Comprehensive reference book. Includes a self-assessment section to identify occupational clues and exploration, work values, home activities, school subjects, work settings, and military occupation specialties and directs user to occupational groupings. Groups thousands of occupations by interests, abilities, and traits required for successful performance. Thorough descriptions of work groups by interests, skills, abilities, education and training, licenses, certifications, income potential, and organizations for further resources. Cross-referenced to DOT codes. Published by U.S. Department of Labor. Updated in 1985.

Occupational Outlook Handbook (OOH)   One of the most widely used career resources. This directory describes approximately 250 occupations covering over 100 million jobs, with an emphasis on careers that are projected to grow rapidly or require lengthy education or training. Information for each occupation includes: nature of work, working conditions, employment training, other qualifications, advancement, job outlook, earnings, related occupations, and sources of additional information. Cross-references the DOT codes under job titles. Summary information on eighty additional occupations. Developed by the U.S. Department of Labor and Bureau of Labor Statistics and updated every two years.

Vocational/Career Inventories and Instruments

The numerous vocational/career inventories and instruments available can measure either personality, interests, or skills as they relate to career possibilities. They don't provide answers; they are tools to help you learn more about yourself and identify career choices. At best, they will expand your ideas about potential careers. Don't allow the results of any inventory or instrument to discourage you if you have a career interest that is not indicated by the results. It will probably take more than one inventory or instrument to get a well-rounded picture of your career self and your options.

The inventories and instruments fall into two categories: those that are administered and interpreted by a counselor and those that are taken and scored on your own.

Counselor-administered inventories and instruments are called restricted instruments, which means that only individuals who are qualified, meeting advanced education and testing requirements, can purchase, administer, and interpret the results. You will find these types of inventories and tests offered privately in one-on-one sessions and in workshops offered through adult and continuing education programs at public schools, colleges, and universities and through counseling centers.

Anyone can use self-administered inventories, which involve taking the inventory, scoring it, and reading additional materials to understand and interpret the results. Some self-administered inventories can be computer scored.

> I don't look to any one self-assessment tool to give me all the information. It's like a puzzle and assessments are the stepping off point. You shouldn't be discouraged by the codes or occupations that are indicated. Assessments are a beginning point to help you jump into the career literature. Use them as a tool and only that.
>
> Karen Romano-Taylor,
> Counselor/Trainer,
> Women's Re-entry Employment Center

The following is a listing of inventories and instruments that are most often recommended by career counselors and are widely available. For each inventory and instrument you will find a general explanation, whether it is counselor- or self-administered, testing time, tips, disadvantages, whom to contact for information, and further readings.

Eureka Skills Inventory

The Eureka Skills Inventory identifies existing skills and skills that you would like to use and matches those skills to a list of 419 occupations.

The Inventory is counselor- or self-administered. Users complete a skills inventory worksheet that evaluates skills in twelve categories, develop a skills record, and list five occupations they'd like using a Eureka occupation list. Skill cards are available, at an additional charge, which describe the skills in more detail and are helpful for users needing more assistance in identifying and categorizing their skills.

The Inventory is turned in for computer scoring. Users receive directions on how to interpret the results, a summary of selected skills related to the Holland Personality Types, clusters of potential occupations and occupational ratings comparing their skills to the skills needed for the occupations.

Testing takes approximately one hour.

TIPS: You will get the best results if you take the time to answer the questions thoroughly. *Disadvantages:* If you are working without counselor assistance, you must interpret the results yourself.

For Information

The California Career Information System
130 33rd St., Rm. 408
Richmond, CA 94804
(415) 235-3883

Further Reading

OOH (see box) and further readings listed for the Self-Directed Search.

The Myers-Briggs Type Indicator

The Myers-Briggs Type Indicator is a personality inventory based on Carl Jung's theory of psychological types. It reports personality preferences on four scales that identify how you prefer to focus attention, how you acquire information, how you make decisions, and how you are oriented toward the outer world. There are sixteen possible types.

The Myers-Briggs Type Indicator (MBTI) is administered by a counselor who will have you answer questions from a test booklet and indicate your answers on a separate answer sheet. There can be no right or wrong answers to the questions, as you will be indicating your preferences. The counselor scores your answer sheet and provides you with a report form that shows your four-letter reported type, your preference score (how consistently you chose one preference over the other), and includes on the reverse side a brief description of all sixteen types. Computer scoring is also available.

Testing takes approximately forty-five minutes.

TIPS: The MBTI will assist you in choosing a career by providing you with an understanding of your work habits and relationships with others. It can complement results from inventories that give specific occupations by considering how your preferences correspond to the work settings of those occupations. There is a short form that is self-scored, but you are better off using the longer forms because errors are possible when scoring the short form and the results of the longer form offer greater reliability. *Disadvantages:* The MBTI is less specific to careers, as it doesn't supply a list of occupations.

For Information

The MBTI is a restricted instrument, and is only available to individuals who meet purchasing requirements. The following organizations provide the MBTI materials and carry additional books and resources.

Center for Applications of
   Psychological Type
2720 NW 6th St.
Gainesville, FL 32609
(800) 777-2278; (904) 375-0160

Consulting Psychologists
   Press, Inc.
3803 E. Bayshore Rd.
Box 10096
Palo Alto, CA 94303
(800) 624-1765; (415) 969-8901.

Otto Kroeger Associates
3605-C Chain Bridge Rd.
Fairfax, VA 22030
(703) 591-MBTI

Type Resources
101 Chestnut St., Ste. 135
Gaithersburg, MD 20877
(301) 963-1283

Further Reading

Gifts Differing
Isabel Briggs Myers
Consulting Psychologists Press, Inc.
3803 E. Bayshore Rd.
Box 10096
Palo Alto, CA 94303
(800) 626-1765; (415) 969-8901

Thorough and upbeat book describing theory behind the MBTI, practical implications of type, and dynamics of type development. Extensive descriptions of the 16 personality preference types. 1980.

Introduction to Type
Isabel Briggs Myers
Consulting Psychologists Press,
   Inc.
[*see above*]
This 32-page booklet provides basic
and comprehensive information on the
theory, preferences, 4 scales, and 16
types, and applications in usefulness
of opposite types, type and relationships, career choice, and problem solving. 1987.

Introduction to Type in
   Organizations
Sandra Hirsch and Jean
   Kummerow
Consulting Psychologist's Press,
   Inc.
[*see above*]

This 32-page booklet gives information about the 4 scales and how they
relate to work situations and communications. information on the four tem-
peraments and 16 types concerning
problem solving, contributions to organizations, leadership style, preferred
work environment, potential pitfalls,
and suggestions for development. 1987.

LIFETypes
Sandra Hirsch and Jean
   Kummerow
Warner Books
666 Fifth Ave.
New York, NY 10103
(800) 638-6460; (212) 484-2900
Extensive, easy-to-read information on
the sixteen preferences.

Self-Directed Search

The Self-Directed Search (SDS) is structured on Holland's Theory (see
box). It helps individuals evaluate interests and abilities, estimate
skills, and identify possible career options.

The SDS is self-administered. Users complete an Assessment Booklet evaluating their occupational daydreams, activities, skills, interests,
and self-estimates. The booklet is scored, and users determine a
three-letter code (Holland Code).

The next step is searching for occupations that match or are related
to this code. The SDS includes *The Occupation Finder*, which lists 1,346

TIPS: When using the SDS, plan on further reading of Holland's Theory and researching additional careers in OOH and
DOT. A College Majors Finder is available to match interests
and abilities indicated by Holland Codes to college majors.
Disadvantages: There are a few combinations of code letters
that don't appear at all, or occur infrequently. Some codes list
four occupations while others list twenty. The SDS is heavily
weighted on past experiences and not as useful as other inventories for individuals who want to make a career change.

occupations by Holland Code along with DOT codes and required education levels.

Testing takes approximately forty-five to sixty minutes.

For Information

Psychological Assessment Resources, Inc.
Box 998
Odessa, FL 33556-9901
(800) 331-TEST; (813) 968-3003

An SDS Specimen Set includes one each of *Assessment Booklet, Occupations Finder, College Majors Finder,* and *You and Your Career.*

Further Reading

Dictionary of Holland Occupational Codes (DHOC)
Gary D. Gottfredson & John D. Holland
Psychological Assessment Resources, Inc.
Box 998
Odessa, FL 33556-9901
(800) 331-TEST; (813) 968-3003

Expanded second edition provides codes for all 12,860 occupational titles contained in the DOT and its supplements. Cross-index shows DOT titles that correspond to each Holland code. 1989.

Making Vocational Choices
John L. Holland
Prentice-Hall, Inc.
Englewood Cliffs, NJ 07632

Provides comprehensive information on John Holland's theory of vocational personalities and work environments and its application to vocational issues in vocational choice, work history, job choices, and occupational achievement. 1985.

Strong Interest Inventory

The Strong Interest Inventory (Strong), formerly known as the Strong-Campbell Interest Inventory, is one of the most widely known and used inventories. It measures your interests with the interests of other individuals who are happily employed in specific occupations and provides a list of occupational titles that reflect clear interest patterns. It is organized by Holland's Theory.

The Strong is counselor-administered. Users complete an assessment booklet and respond to likes and dislikes on a wide range of occupations, occupational activities, leisure activities, school subjects, types of people, and personal characteristics.

The Strong must be computer-scored. Several types of reports are available: the Profile Report is a comprehensive summary of the client's results; the Interpretive Report is a brief interpretation of the client's scores; and the Strong Expanded Interpretive Report is a comprehensive report that gives job descriptions, educational requirements, and employment outlooks for career interests based on the client's results of the Strong.

Testing takes approximately thirty to forty-five minutes.

TIPS: Work through the instrument quickly to achieve the best results. In the occupations section, rely on your first impressions rather than how well you could do the job or how much money the job typically pays. An experienced counselor can help you interpret the results and identify a variety of work environments that are compatible with your interests. *Disadvantages:* You identify your interests in a variety of occupations and you might now understand what some of those occupations are. If you have too many or too few likes and dislikes, it might affect your profile.

For Information

The Strong is a restricted instrument and is only available to individuals who meet purchasing requirements. The following organization carries the Strong instrument and additional resources and books.

Consulting Psychologists Press, Inc.
3803 E. Bayshore Rd.
Box 10096
Palo Alto, CA 94303
(800) 624-1765; (415) 969-8901

Further Reading

Career Development Guide for Use With the Strong
Sally Brew
Consulting Psychologists Press, Inc.
3803 E. Bayshore Rd.
Box 10096
Palo Alto, CA 94303
(800) 624-1765; (415) 969-8901
24-page workbook containing exercises designed to help focus interests in a career direction using the Strong results.

Introduction to the Strong in Organizational Settings
Sandra Krebs Hirsh & Tom Vessey
Consulting Psychologists Press
[*see above*]
Booklet designed to show how to apply Strong concepts and results to career planning, teamwork, communication, work environment, and person-job fit.

Vocational Preference Inventory

The Vocational Preference Inventory (VPI), composed entirely of occupational titles, is considered to be another instrument based on the RIASEC Theory. It is a brief inventory and is recommended as a useful supplement to the Self-Directed Search and other interest inventories.
   The VPI is counselor-administered.
   Testing takes approximately fifteen to thirty minutes.

> TIPS: The VPI should be interpreted by psychologists, vocational counselors, and personnel workers with at least one year of graduate training and a substantial understanding of tests and personality. *Disadvantages:* The VPI is most beneficial when used in conjunction with other assessment inventories.

For Information

The VPI is a restricted instrument and only available to individuals who meet purchasing requirements. The following organization carries the VPI instrument and additional resources.

Psychological Assessment Resources, Inc.
Box 998
Odessa, FL 33556
(800) 331-TEST; (813) 968-3003

How to Locate Testing and Counseling Services

The following resources identify organizations, counselors, and workshops that offer testing and counseling services.

Directory of Counseling Services
International Association of
 Counseling Services
5999 Stevenson Ave.
Alexandria, VA 22304
(703) 823-9800, ext. 385
Directory includes private and college counseling centers located in the United States.

*The National Business
 Employment Weekly*
Published by Dow Jones & Co.
Available at your newsstand or
 library or call (800) JOB-HUNT
 or (212) 808-6792.
Offers a biweekly Calendar of Events by region across the United States. It publicizes events and services for job seekers that are available either free or at nominal cost.

*The National Directory of
 Certified Counselors*
National Board of Certified
 Counselors (NBCC)
5999 Stevenson Ave.
Alexandria, VA 22304
(703) 461-6222

Directory includes National Certified Counselors, National Certified Career Counselors, and Certified Clinical Mental Health Counselors listed alphabetically and by state.

What Color Is Your Parachute?
Richard Nelson Bolles
Ten Speed Press
Box 7123
Berkeley, CA 94707
(415) 845-8414
Includes listings of places that counsel anyone, help for women (many serve men too), and directories of career counseling services in various cities and states. 1991.

*Women's Organizations: A
 National Directory*
Martha Merrill Doss
Garrett Park Press
Garrett Park, MD 20896
(301) 946-2553
Lists hundreds of organizations, many providing career, guidance, and employment services. Organized alphabetically by organization name; includes an index by category. 1986.

For additional resources, contact career services at your local college or university or career programs through adult and continuing education programs or your local government.

Doing It Yourself

A part of knowing yourself is knowing whether you have the ability and perseverance to work though the self-analysis process alone, or whether you need the structure and discipline of a formal workshop or private counseling.

If you have the tenacity to work through exercises and programs, there are excellent books, workbooks, and computer software to assist you in this endeavor. This section provides resources, where to locate them, and a short description to help you choose what will work for you.

Computer Software

Interactive software involves you in the process, asks questions, and requires a response. Interactive career software programs are available for individual and institutional use. Software for individuals can be purchased at stores and through catalogs. Software for institutions is available for use at career development and placement centers in colleges and universities and at some large public libraries. Career counselors usually assist you with institutional software. Check your local colleges, universities, and public libraries for programs and availability.

For Individual Use

Career Navigator
Drake Beam Morin, Inc.
100 Park Ave.
New York, NY 10017
(212) 692-5813

Easy-to-use career exploration and job search program for the IBM PC. Contains screen information, quizzes, exercises, values sort-cards, and an excellent handbook with instructions, job search directions, and numerous resources. Includes word processing program for letter and résumé writing.

Federal Occupational and Career Information System (FOCIS)
National Technical Information Service (NTIS)
5285 Port Royal Rd.
Springfield, VA 22161
(703) 487-4650

Excellent program assisting the white-collar job seeker in identifying interests and learning about job opportunities in the Executive Branch of the federal government. Identifies opportunities by over 100 college majors and lists up to 10 specific occupations for each major. Lists job descriptions, minimum qualifications required, grades and salary information, agencies that hire the occupation and where located, and number currently employed for 360 occupations. Alphabetical list of hiring agencies, by subdivisions, regions, states, and cities, providing agency descriptions and addresses. Can print information by screen, not file, using print screen key. Systems requirements include IBM PC or compatible with a high density (1.2 megabyte) 5 ¼-inch disk drive.

The Occupational Outlook Handbook
Career Development Software, Inc.
Box 5379
Vancouver, WA 98668
(206) 696-3529

Excellent career exploratory program featuring an assessment inventory, 301 careers from the OOH. Cross-references these careers to the DOT and the Worker Trait Group System. Inventory includes activities you enjoy, type and length of training preferences, and skills, and prints out results of your personal inventory. Program searches for and lists careers that match your preferences. Provided for each career area description, related work activities, related work situations, related occupations, employment outlook, types of training, length of training, necessary skills, contacts for further information worker trait group code, DOT code, and OOH category. Using drop-down menus, provides inventory of careers and related careers. Available for both the IBM PC and Apple II. 1990.

Skills of the Future
Career Development Software,
   Inc.
[*see above*]
Interesting program for IBM PC containing skills inventory and information on desirable future skills. Choose the long skill inventory version of forty-two questions to assess skill interests in doing, investigating, creating, helping, influencing, and organizing skills of the future and receive profile (and option to print) of your skills. Provides information on careers in high demand using these skills, descriptions, college majors, major skills involved, and national associations. 1986.

For Institutional Use

*DISCOVER for Adult Learners
   (DAL)*
American College Testing Center
230 Schilling Circle
Hunt Valley, MD 21301
(301) 628-8000

An interactive career guidance program designed for adults. Modules include: weathering change, assessing yourself and identifying alternatives, gathering occupational information, making decisions, drafting educational plans, and getting a job.

Sigi Plus
Educational Testing Service
Princeton, NJ 08541
(800) 257-7444
An easy-to-use career guidance system that helps you plan your career. Contains modules to assess work-related values, interests, and activities that are important; identifies options to explore; provides information on skills, educational requirements, and training for those options; and teaches decision-making strategies to help you work towards goal achievement.

Computer On-Line Services

The Career Center
New England Center for Career Development
Box 297
Hooksett, NH 03106
(603) 622-5587

The Career Center is an electronic career development service with professional, educational, career, and employment assistance and information for on-line subscribers. It is available for Quantum networks, and accessible on PC Link for the IBM and IBM compatible users, AO for Macintosh users, and Promenade for IBM PS/1 users. It offers subscribers career counseling, both individual and group; career conferences, lectures, and discussions, twice a month; timely career development articles that can be downloaded; bulletin boards for questions; résumé templates; collection of employment letters; *Career Focus 2000*, a self-instructional program of career guidance that helps users identify a career direction; occupational library with over 1,000 different occupations in the United States; large collection of U.S. employers including name, address, type of company, product or service line, contact person, and number of employees; large collection of resources aiding users in advancing their education, career, and employment.

Further Reading

Books

Career planning books offering occupational information are invaluable as you pursue occupational exploration, even if you already have extensive work experience. The following books are the best resources, as they are written clearly and offer insight into careers and provide additional information to further your exploration.

College Majors and Careers
Paul Phifer
Garrett Park Press
Garrett Park, MD 20896
(301) 946-2553
Excellent guide that profiles 60 college majors, related occupations, minimum of education required, related avocational and leisure-time activities, related skills, values and personal attributes, organizations, sources for further exploration, and definitions for 400 not-as-well-known occupations. 1987.

Encyclopedia of Careers and Vocational Guidance, Eighth Edition
Edited by William E. Hopke
J. G. Fergusen Publishing Co.
200 W. Monroe St.
Chicago, IL 60606
(312) 580-5480
Four-volume set describes 450 occupations as to nature of work, entry requirements, training and educational requirements, working conditions, advancement opportunities, earnings, and sources of additional information. One volume devoted to new, emerging, or changing technical careers. 1990.

Dream Jobs
Robert W. Bly & Gary Blake
John Wiley & Sons, Inc.
605 3rd Ave.
New York, NY 10158
(212) 850-6000
Provides comprehensive information for careers in advertising, biotechnology, cable TV, computers, consulting, public relations, telecommunications, training and development, and travel. Includes general descriptions, what it takes, getting started, what to read, your first big break, what to shoot for, how you'll know when you've made it, and numerous resources for further exploration. While the information is valuable, some of it is out of date. 1983.

Professional Careers Sourcebook
Kathleen M. Savage & Charity Anne Dorgan, Eds.
Gale Research, Inc.
835 Penobscot Bldg.
Detroit, MI 48226-4094
(313) 961-2242; (800) 347-GALE
Excellent directory providing job descriptions for 111 careers requiring college degrees or specialized education. Designed as a companion of OOH. Includes: employment outlook and salaries, descriptive listings for directories of educational programs, special training programs, standards/certification agencies, professional associations and related organizations, professional reference works and trade periodicals, print, audio, and film resources, career guides, test guides, awards, scholarships, grants, fellowships, and professional meetings and conventions. 1990.

Workbooks

Workbooks contain both text and exercises and often include forms for you to write on as you complete the exercises. The following clearly written workbooks will motivate and inspire you in identifying your interests and planning for your career.

How to Create a Picture of Your Ideal Job or Next Career
Richard N. Bolles
Ten Speed Press
Box 7123
Berkeley, CA 94707
(415) 845-8414
Exercises that help you identify what you'd like in a physical, spiritual, or emotional setting; skills, people, information, things you'd like to use skills with; salary and immediate and long-range goals. From *What Color is Your Parachute?*; replaces *The Quick Job Hunting Map.* 1989.

The New Quick Job Hunting Map
Richard N. Bolles
Ten Speed Press
Box 7123
Berkeley, CA 94707
(415) 845-8414
Exercises to identify your skills and gifts and where you would be happiest using them. Beginning and advanced versions. From *What Color is Your Parachute?* 1989, 1990.

Training for Life
Fred Hecklinger & Bernadette Black
Kendall/Hunt Publishing Co.
2460 Kerper Blvd.
Box 539
Dubuque, IA 52001
Easy-to-follow exercises to identify skills, interests, values, and plan short- and long-term career and lifestyle goals. Packed with information and resources for career change, revitalization, and transitions. 1990.

What Color is Your Parachute?
Richard N. Bolles
Ten Speed Press
Box 7123
Berkeley, CA 94707
One of the most comprehensive career planning resources. Inspirational text and extensive resources to help you identify, plan, and find your career. Updated annually. 1991.

Wishcraft
Barbara Sher
Ballantine
201 E. 50th St.
New York, NY 10022
(212) 572-2620; (800) 733-3000
Identify hidden strengths, set goals, and develop a timetable and network to achieve your career goals. Lots of exercises, personal experiences, and support to see you through. 1986.

Your Hidden Skills: Clues to Careers and Future Pursuits
Henry G. Pearson
Mowry Press
Wayland, MA 01778
Identifies skills based on knowledge, know-how, or subject matter and "tran-skills" (those that can be transferred easily from one job to another). Contains numerous lists of skills and exercises that help you identify and organize your skills, define your priorities (likes and dislikes), translate job tasks into transkills, explore careers, and sample career directions. 1981.

Piecing the Puzzle

You're going to accumulate a great deal of information about yourself in the self-analysis process. How can you integrate it all? For starters, begin by looking for patterns in your skills and interests. What occupations or work environments tie in to your skills and interests? Explore these by researching careers in books and periodicals. Your public library will be of assistance, as will the career libraries and centers at local colleges and universities, and the guidance offices and career centers in local high schools.

Investigate the services that your present employer offers. Many organizations provide their employees with career planning or career management services including counseling, workbooks, computer programs, and a variety of personalized activity plans.

Attend panel programs and career exploratory programs that are of interest to you. These programs are typically conducted by one or more professionals in a specific career area who can share with you a typical workday, the pros and cons of their career, current salaries, educational requirements, and sources for additional information. The programs are sponsored by adult and continuing education programs, professional and trade associations, local governments, libraries, nonprofit, community, and social service organizations, and counseling agencies. Look for program announcements in the weekly and business calendars of your local paper.

Set up informational meetings with individuals presently working in jobs that appeal to you or who hire for these jobs. Use the meeting to gather information about what the job is really like, the opportunities, and required skills and education. Plan to take up no more than forty-five minutes of the person's time.

Prepare for the meeting by choosing questions that will give you information about the profession enabling you to decide whether to pursue this career. For example, ask:

> "What are the greatest problems and challenges facing your industry?"
> "What skills, education, and experience are required for this job?"

Confirm whether you have the qualifications for the job and if not, get suggestions on how you can better qualify.

Ask for the names of additional contacts who can provide more information about opportunities in the field or industry so you can continue your exploration. Request recommendations for additional reading, training, and educational resources.

Send a follow-up note expressing your gratitude to the person for having taken the time to speak with you and provide you with information and resources. You can include a copy of your résumé. The following resource details how to make the most from informational meetings.

Information Interviewing: What It Is and How to Use It in Your Career
Martha Stoodley
Garrett Park Press
Garrett Park, MD 20896
(301) 946-2553
Useful guide identifying techniques for making contacts and suggestions for obtaining the most useful information from the interviews. 1990.

Chapter 3

Boosting Your Options

Keeping up with business and occupational changes can be an awesome task, but it's an essential one if you are to survive and succeed in the workplace.

Technological innovations coupled with a shift from an industrial economy to a service-based economy have broadened career opportunities while making others obsolete. Organizations are moving away from hierarchical forms of management, reducing middle management positions and, consequently, job opportunities. You'll need a thorough knowledge of business, industry, and career trends to chart a career course with potential for advancement.

> Business doesn't seem to stay the same anymore, it always seems to be in a state of flux. I think that state of flux is normal, not abnormal. This change and chaos and lack of normalcy is going to be normalcy in the future.
>
> Bruce Crockett,
> President and Chief Operating Officer,
> World Division, Comsat Corporation

Business Trends

Business trends have far-reaching implications for career stability and opportunities. Savvy individuals use trends to predict careers and industries that are on the move, heading toward expansion and openings. You too should try to assess business trends when making your career plans. For instance, consider how these trends affect you today.

• The service-producing sector is projected to experience an increase of approximately 18 million new jobs in the next decade. Futurists are forecasting that by the year 2000, 95 percent of all jobs will be in the service industries.

• Manufacturing employment is predicted to shrink slightly.

• Technology has dramatically changed the workplace. Technological advancements and changes will continue throughout the next decade, significantly affecting the way business is done. Employees must be willing to be retrained and to commit themselves to lifelong learning if they are to keep up with new technology.

• Employment opportunities are moving from larger to smaller organizations. More opportunities and new jobs will be with smaller firms employing less than 100 workers. *CAM Report* stated that "Fortune 500 companies have slashed 3.5 million jobs from payrolls since 1989, but small business generated 20 million new jobs during the same period." [1]

• Organizations are becoming more customer-care–oriented, identifying and understanding customer requirements and delivering what the customer wants. Employers are seeking employees who are customer-service–oriented.

• Global changes in political structures and trade have opened a multitude of international opportunities. "American exports clearly have the potential to grow further as new international markets develop and commerce becomes increasingly global," states *Nation's Business*.[2]

• Entrepreneurship, the creation and growth of small businesses, is an area that has experienced significant growth and is predicted to increase steadily throughout the decade. The Census Bureau reports that women-owned businesses were the fastest growing sector in the economy, growing four times faster than all businesses, increasing 57 percent between 1982 and 1987. Approximately 30 percent of all U.S. businesses are currently owned by women and the Small Business Administration conservatively predicts that women will own approximately 37 percent of all U.S. businesses by the year 2000.

Further Reading

The business community experiences constant change and you need to keep abreast of what's coming in and what's going out. The following newspapers, newsletters, and magazines are your best bets for keeping pace with the business community.

1. *CAM Report*, 13, no. 10 (March 1990): 1. As quoted in *U.S. News & World Report*, 26 Sept. 1989.
2. *Nation's Business*, September 1990, p. 29.

Newspapers

Crain's Chicago Business
Crain Communications, Inc.
  (Chicago)
740 N. Rush St.
Chicago, IL 60611-2590
(312) 649-5270
Weekly periodical covering business, labor, and related issues in Chicago.

Crain's Detroit Business
Crain Communications, Inc.
  (Detroit)
965 E. Jefferson Ave.
Detroit, MI 48207-9966
(313) 446-0459
Weekly periodical covering business, labor, and related issues in Detroit.

Crain's New York Business
Crain Communications, Inc.
  (New York)
965 E. Jefferson Ave.
Detroit, MI 48207-9966
(212) 210-0100
Weekly periodical covering business, labor, and related issues in New York.

The New York Times
229 W. 43 St.
New York, NY 10036
(212) 556-1234
Daily general newspaper.

The Wall Street Journal
Dow Jones & Co., Inc.
200 Liberty St.
New York, NY 10281
(212) 416-2000
National business and financial newspaper, published Monday through Friday.

The Washington Post
1150 15th St. NW
Washington, DC 20071
(202) 334-6000
Daily general newspaper. Special Monday business section.

Newsletters

The Kiplinger Washington Letter
The Kiplinger Washington Editors
1729 H St. NW
Washington, DC 20006-3938
(202) 887-6400
Weekly newsletter covering business news and issues.

Magazines

Business Week
McGraw-Hill, Inc.
1221 Ave. of the Americas
New York, NY 10020
(212) 512-3598
Weekly business news magazine.

Forbes
60 Fifth Ave.
New York, NY 10011
(212) 620-2200
Business magazine published every other week.

Fortune
Time, Inc.
Time & Life Bldg.
1271 Avenue of the Americas
New York, NY 10020
(212) 522-1212
Business magazine published 27 times a year in regional and demographic editions.

INC.
38 Commercial Wharf
Boston, MA 02110
(617) 248-8000

Monthly business magazine for manager's of growing companies with up to $100 million in sales.

Kiplinger's Personal Finance Magazine
1729 H St. NW
Washington, DC 20006
(202) 887-6400

Monthly personal finance magazine including business and career projections and recommendations.

Money
Time & Life Bldg.
1271 Avenue of the Americas
New York, NY 10020
(800) 633-9970

Monthly general business and financial magazine with periodic career articles.

Nation's Business
1615 H St. NW
Washington, DC 20062
(202) 463-5650

Monthly magazine published by the U.S. Chamber of Commerce for owners and managers of businesses.

Newsweek
444 Madison Ave.
New York, NY 10022
(212) 350-4547

Weekly news magazine including reports on business and economic issues.

Time
Time, Inc.
Time & Life Bldg.
1271 Avenue of the Americas
New York, NY 10020
(212) 522-1212

Weekly news magazine including reports on business and economic issues.

Indexes

Business Index
Information Access Co.
362 Lakeside Dr.
Foster City, CA 94404
(800) 227-8431

A monthly index of over 700 regional and national business, trade, and management journals, including *The Wall Street Journal* and the business and financial section of *The New York Times*. Available on microfilm or on-line.

Business Periodical Index
H. W. Wilson Co.
950 University Ave.
Bronx, NY 10452
(212) 588-8400

A monthly (except for August) index of business and industry subjects from over 300 business publications. Quarterly and annual cumulations.

The New York Times Index
The New York Times Co.
229 W. 43 St.
New York, NY 10036
(212) 556-1234

A monthly index of pages from *The New York Times* including a cumulative index at the end of each year. Briefly summarizes all items, reports, and indexes, cross-referenced by subject and name.

Predicasts F & S Index United States
11001 Cedar Ave.
Cleveland, OH 44106
(216) 795-3000; (800) 321-6388

A quarterly index of company, product, and industry information from 750 financial publications, including business-oriented newspapers, trade magazines, and special reports.

Reader's Guide to
  Periodical Literature
H. W. Wilson Co.
[see above]
Monthly (except for January and August) index of approximately 200 general interest magazines, including career and business publications.

The Wall Street Journal Index
Dow Jones & Co., Inc.
200 Liberty St.
New York, NY 10281
(212) 416-2000
Publishes a monthly and annual index of The Wall Street Journal. Includes corporate and general business news.

Industry Trends

While job opportunities will continue in manufacturing and in slower-growth industries, all the new jobs created and the best possibilities will be found in service industries and new technologies. Service industries differ from manufacturing in that they create economic value without producing a tangible product. New and advanced technology in information storage and processing, communications, advanced materials, biotechnologies, and superconductivity significantly affect operations as well as job opportunities.

Where are some hot career areas? You'll find them in health care, telecommunications, computers, and education. The next section describes trends in each of these areas and offers an industry expert's forecast of where you can find the opportunities.

Applicable periodicals and professional associations are included to keep you updated on industry trends. Locate additional periodicals in:

Gale Directory of Publications and Broadcast Media
835 Penobscot Bldg.
Detroit, MI 48226-4094
(313) 961-2242; (800) 347-GALE
Directory of newspapers, magazines, and journals. includes names, addresses, phone numbers, and short descriptions. Includes index. 1990.

Health Care

Health care is a field with diverse opportunities offering flexibility, competitive salaries, and, due to growing demands, a stable and secure career. The Bureau of Labor Statistics has identified seven of the ten fastest growing occupations as being in the health care field.

According to the Bureau of Labor Statistics (*Monthly Labor Review*, November 1989), "health care will continue to be one of the most important industry sectors in the economy. . . . Employment in the private health services industries rose from 4.4 million in 1976 (or one of every eighteen wage and salary jobs) to 7.1 million in 1988 (one of every fifteen), and is projected to grow to 10.1 million by 2000 (representing one of twelve jobs). The increase in health care jobs between 1988 and 2000 accounts for more than one-sixth of the total payroll job growth projected."

Health Care Trends

Health care is experiencing a shifting of service from inpatient (hospital) to out-patient (ambulatory) care. Jobs in hospitals have experienced the slowest growth (an increase of approximately 10 percent between 1982 and 1988), while jobs in doctors' offices rose 36 percent, and jobs in out-patient facilities rose 81 percent. Hospitals, employing 3.3 million workers, are still the largest employer in the health care industry. Figure 1 demonstrates employment gains and future opportunities in private health industries.

Hospital stays are being shortened, the population is aging, and technological advances make for a dynamic environment as the health care industry targets services and support to meet the growing and changing needs of the consumer. While hospital jobs are slowly increasing, jobs in the offices of health care practitioners are increasing faster.

Rich Stacy, Director, Human Resource Development, INOVA Health Systems, speaks about health care career options:

> There are so many career options now available, but there are not as many people entering the health care field. That is why there is a shortage—not necessarily of nurses but of nurses practicing in the direct patient care environment; they have left the field to do other things. They sell pharmaceuticals, they sell information systems, they go into entirely different careers that have no correlation to health care. The same is true in a lot of other areas. People get burned out and just leave. Health care is a twenty-four-hour-a-day, 365-day-a-year kind of field.
>
> It's interesting that although technology is constantly changing, it doesn't have a negative impact on careers. Instead of discontinuing technology, we're simply adding new forms. Radiology is a good example. We have moved from the regular diagnostic radiology to the CAT scan to the MRI but we still use all three for different treatment modalities.
>
> Home care—out-patient care and thearapy—is a big, big business. An offshoot of the visiting nurse, we're now talking about a broad spectrum of care from home health aides to

Figure 1. Profile of private health industries, 1988–2000 (in thousands).

Industry	Employment			Annual Rate of Change	
	1988	2000	Gain, 1988–2000	Employment	Output
Total health services	7,144	10,139	2,995	3.0	3.3
Offices of health practitioners...........	1,850	2,810	960	3.5	2.7
Offices of physicians	1,146	1,843	697	4.1	—
Offices of dentists	486	575	89	1.0	—
Other	218	391	173	5.0	—
Nursing and personal care facilities	1,319	1,907	588	3.1	3.9
Hospitals..................	3,300	4,245	945	2.1	3.3
Outpatient facilities and other health services	675	1,177	502	4.7	4.6
Medical and dental labs	149	239	90	4.0	—
Outpatient care facilities................	266	475	209	4.9	—
Other	260	463	203	4.9	—
Note: Dash indicates data not available.					

Source: *Monthly Labor Review* (Washington D.C.: U.S. Department of Labor, Bureau of Labor Statistics, November 1989, p. 29).

highly trained nurses and other technicians providing out-patient therapy, physical therapy, and occupational therapy.

Some growth will be seen in nursing homes, but we now call them care centers. We'll see different levels of care being rendered and you won't have to be elderly to be in a care center. It will be an alternative place for someone who is ready to leave the hospital but has no home to go to.

Many procedures are now being done in out-patient surgery facilities, where you check in in the morning and go home in the afternoon.

Health care has become extremely flexible in staffing and assignments to continue to attract and retain employees.

Out-patient trends now offer 9 to 5, Monday to Friday work schedules.

Health care is no different from any other industry trying to be innovative—bringing on new product lines to meet the consumer's requirements for both quality and price, service, and convenience. More and more people are realizing that health care is a business, taking care of people who are ill and need to have something done. You still have to have a little bit of altruism to work in health care, but we are still a business.

Resources

The following professional associations and professional and trade periodicals will keep you informed of specific trends and opportunities.

Professional Associations

American Hospital Association (AHA)
840 Lake Shore Dr.
Chicago, IL 60611
(312) 280-6000
National association for individuals and health care institutions. Extensive health care administration library. Conducts various research and educational projects in health care field. Publishes annual *Guide to the Health Care Field.*

National Health Council (NHC)
350 Fifth Ave., Ste. 1118
New York, NY 10118
(212) 268-8900
National association with mission to improve the health of the nation. Distributes *200 Ways to Put Your Talents to Work* in the Health Field and other materials on health careers.

Professional and Trade Periodicals

Hospitals
American Hospital Publishers, Inc.
211 E. Chicago Ave., Ste. 700
Chicago, IL 60611
(312) 440-6800
Health administration magazine, published every other week, for health care executives.

Modern Healthcare
Crain Communications
740 N. Rush St.
Chicago, IL 60611
(312) 649-5200
Weekly periodical containing articles on a broad range of topics in the health care field.

Telecommunications

Telecommunications innovations in fiber optic cable networks, satellite communications, digital switching systems, advanced office automation, and digital transmission have moved us far away from the plain old telephone (POT). Telecommunications have brought the world closer and closer together by electronically communicating information by fax, telex, cellular phone, cable television, electronic mail, online databases, and consumer databases.

The telecommunications industry, a growth industry for the 1990s and beyond, is experiencing tremendous growth domestically, and even faster growth internationally. Satellites and fiber optics (glass cables that run on the ocean bottom), are shrinking the world by handling hundreds of thousands of simultaneous phone calls.

There will be excellent job opportunities for electrical engineers, electronic and mechanical technicians, computer programmers, marketing and financial specialists, writers, videographers, educators, news reporters, announcers, computer animators, and graphic artists.

The Bureau of Labor Statistics predicts that jobs for telephone communications managers and administrators will grow about 18 percent in the next decade. "The increase in the demand for managers is related to the growing number of services provided through the telephone network and to the many small service and specialty firms that are appearing within this industry." [3] Technologial change affects other occupations, including the number of jobs for computer systems analysts, which is anticipated to grow by 50 percent within the next decade.

Figure 2. Outlook for telephone communications employment in selected occupations, 1988–2000.

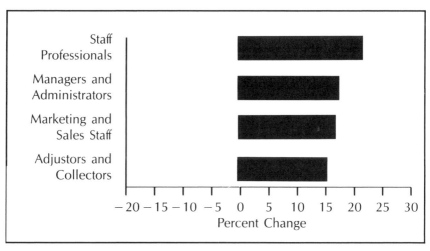

Source: Adapted from *Outlook for Technology and Labor in Telephone Communications* (Washington, D.C.: U.S. Department of Labor, Bureau of Labor Statistics, July 1990, p. 14). (Based on the moderate projection.)

3. *Outlook for Technology and Labor in Telephone Communications* (Washington, D.C.: U.S. Department of Labor, Bureau of Labor Statistics, July 1990), p. 13.

Figure 2 projects increased telephone communications employment opportunities for staff professionals, managers and administrators, marketing and sales, and adjustors and collectors.

Telecommunications Trends

Within a decade, all communications are going to be conducted via satellite and fiber optic cables. New industry innovations include mobile phones, high-definition television, and caller identification. Integrated systems digital networks (ISDNs) will combine voice, data, and image over a single telephone line.

According to Bruce Crockett, President and Chief Operating Officer, Comsat Corporation:

Communications is a great industry to get involved in because it is going to explode.

International communications is growing at close to 20 percent a year right now and it will continue. Eastern Europe is like the last frontier, it hasn't really opened up yet. Between the Soviet Union and the United States there are twenty-eight satellite circuits. Between Puerto Rico and the United States, there are 7,000; between the United Kingdom and the United States, there are 4,000; between France and the United States, there are 3,000.

Satellites and fiber optics have made it possible to do things that people thought were seemingly impossible. Eventually there will be a wide band with fiber optic cable into every home and over it you will get your telephone calls, your own personalized fax number, your television, and you will be able to choose from thousands of simultaneous television programs. You can go to night school at home, [and learn] everything that you can think of in terms of information processing in one form or another, from banking to newspapers. Eventually, all this information will be on your CRT and you can sit there in the morning and read the newspaper on your video screen. Everything that you think of as information processing is communications and it will affect many industries such as movies, communications, computers, television, and radio.

Opportunities exist in mobile communications via satellite such as ships at sea, airplanes, and land mobile applications. Potentially, we'll be able to track truck drivers and always know exactly where they are.

Telecommunications is a chaotic environment and so much change creates a lot of opportunities.

Resources

The following professional associations and professional and trade periodicals will keep you informed of future trends and opportunities.

Professional Associations

You won't find general associations providing basic information for this industry. Look for specialized associations. If you're interested in the mobile telephone industry, check out the National Association of Cellular Agents, or if you're interested in satellite communications, check out the Satellite Broadcasting and Communications associations. Look for other associations in directories under the listing *Telecommunications*.

Professional and Trade Periodicals

Communications Daily
2115 Ward Ct. NW
Washington, DC 20037
(202) 872-9200
Daily publication covering entire telecommunications industry.

Communications News
7500 Old Oak Blvd.
Cleveland, OH 44130
(216) 243-8100
Monthly publication covering voice,
video, and data communication management.

*CommunicationsWeek
  International*
CMP Publications, Inc.
600 Community Dr.
Manhasset, NY 11030
(516) 562-5000
Communications newspaper, published
every other week, for managers and
international executives.

Telecommunications
Horizon House
685 Canton St.
Norwood, MA 02062
(617) 769-9750
Monthly magazine on data communications and international communications.

Computers

The Bureau of Labor Statistics predicts the computer services industry to be the fastest growing segment of the business services industry as well as of the economy. The Bureau projects that employment in this sector will grow 4.9 percent a year, reaching 1.2 million by the year 2000.

Computer hardware, the equipment side of the business, will experience growth in customized computer systems but the most new opportunities will be in computer software.

What is the proverbial distinction between software and hardware? It is the distinction between programs and machines—between long, complicated sequences of instructions and the physical machines which carry them out. I like to think of software as "anything you could send over the telephone lines," and hardware as "anything else." A piano is hardware, but printed music is software. A telephone set is hardware but a telephone number is software.

Douglas R. Hofstadter,
American computer scientist

Computer Trends

C language, used in programming in UNIX and OS/2, has become the programming language most in demand.

UNIX, a transportable operating system, is very attractive to users as it provides the ability to create less brand-oriented networks of computer systems and has an advantage—software in C language will run on any hardware.

The most promising careers are as operations research analysts, computer systems analysts, programmers, database designers, and in systems support and services and systems integration.

Wade Robinson, Director, Planning and Staffing, Defense Systems, UNISYS Corporation, says:

What's happened in the industry is that hardware manufacturers have oversold the product. Many users have enough hardware, but [no one has] developed enough sophisticated software to put that hardware to greater use. So you've got hardware out there spinning through cycles.

The biggest industry right now is software packages, which are essentially efficiency and productivity tools. So it's relatively simple to see where the industry is going. I wouldn't emphasize the hardware business but instead, a specific side of the software business.

The big challenge is to try and find some emerging technology, something that is not there yet. Eight years ago there was UNIX. If you had the ability to identify where that product was going in the industry, you could position yourself for success. You need to find a product that is in the same development cycle that UNIX was in five years ago.

There is something out there right now that is the UNIX of the late 1990s.

You have to keep up with the industry, be proactive, and read all the industry literature you can. The big challenge is finding an emerging technology and getting yourself in on the ground floor technically, so that when the demand for it arises, you'll be ahead of the market.

Resources

The following professional associations and professional and trade periodicals will keep you informed of future trends and opportunities.

Professional Associations

Association for Computing
  Machinery
11 W. 42nd St., 3rd fl.
New York, NY 10036
(212) 869-7440
National association for individuals interested in computing and data processing careers. Focuses on specific computer issues through over thirty special interest groups.

Professional and Trade Periodicals

Computerworld
IDG Communications
375 Cochituate Rd.
Box 9171
Framingham, MA 01701
(617) 879-0700
Weekly publication for the computer industry providing news and company and product information.

Datamation
Cahners Publishing
249 W. 17th St.
New York, NY 10011
(212) 645-0067
Bimonthly publication providing articles on mini- and microcomputers and programming languages.

Education

We've all read about the exodus of teachers from the education profession and the closing of elementary and secondary schools due to decreasing enrollments in the early 1980s.

But the downward trend of school enrollments was reversed as children of the baby-boom generation began attending elementary school later in the 1980s. The increased student population, as well as other trends, has made education a growing field with a potential addition of 1.2 million jobs over the next decade. As these children grow and move through intermediate and secondary school, according to the Bureau of Labor Statistics, "employment in state and local government education is expected to climb to 8.3 million by the year 2000." [4]

Education Trends

The teacher core has decreased, partially due to the migration away from teaching, coupled with a large percentage of teachers reaching retirement. However, the demand for teachers has increased, with particular specialties already experiencing shortages. Here's why:

- The school population has changed, with a growing number of blacks, Hispanics, and immigrants significantly increasing the non-English-speaking student population.
- Many states are reviewing and considering changes to the school year, perhaps even eliminating summer vacations.
- Preschool education for three- and four-year-olds has and will continue to grow, creating a demand for preschool teachers, while kindergarten, although not mandatory, has now become the rule almost everywhere.
- Parents in the workplace have created a demand for extended care. School systems are beginning to fill this need, offering enrichment programs starting at 7 A.M. and lasting until 7 P.M.
- Teacher salaries have increased, making education a more attractive career.

According to Senta Raizen, Director, National Center for Improving Science Education:

> There is already an increasing demand for teachers in particular fields. Secondary-school mathematics, physics, chemistry and earth science, special education, and bilingual education are fields already experiencing shortages.
>
> All sorts of specialists will be needed to make education effective for special populations. Bilingual teachers and specialists for children with disabilities are in demand as well as people who can develop curriculums or plan for special populations.
>
> There are educational opportunities outside the traditional teaching fields. Apprenticeship programs (similar to Germany's) that combine education at work and in the

4. *Monthly Labor Review* (Washington, D.C.: U.S. Department of Labor, Bureau of Labor Statistics, November 1989), p. 31.

classroom are being discussed to meet the shortages in the skilled labor pool. There are opportunities for people who can develop good training and educational programs to be shared between schools and industry and private businesses.

Private-industry training is a growing field. We'll need training programs for the existing work force, not just on-the-job training that is specific to a particular job, but programs that make workers function better in general, such as stress reduction, quality control, and effectiveness programs.

The commitment to lifelong learning opens opportunities for individuals who can develop relationships between industry and higher education, whether at a two- or four-year institution, offering programs that can be bought by private industry for their employees, reducing the need for in-house development.

Individuals interested in education should think about making themselves more competitive by acquiring special skills that meet current shortages. Good managers for large, urban school systems are in demand. So are teachers to work with the economically disadvantaged, hearing disabled, visually disabled, and children whose first language is not English. If you develop a special interest where there are current or anticipated shortages, you'll be snapped up.

Check with the central or personnel office of your county or local educational jurisdiction and ask, "What kinds of positions do you anticipate will be in short supply in the next three or four years?" Inquire about state and district requirements as well. While administrative and managerial functions experience competition in other sectors, there are always opportunities in education at the administrative level; for example, good accountants are always in short supply.

Resources

The following professional associations and professional and trade periodicals will keep you informed of future trends and opportunities.

Professional Associations

American Federation of Teachers (AFT)
555 New Jersey Ave. NW
Washington, DC 20001
(202) 879-4400

Offers teachers and other educational employees support in organizing, collective bargaining, and information on educational issues.

Association for Supervision and Curriculum Development (ASCD)
1250 N. Pitt St.
Alexandria, VA
(703) 549-9110
Offers publications on education news and trends, professional development, hands-on-training, and networking opportunities.

National Education Association
1201 16th St. NW
Washington, DC 20036
(202) 833-4000
Professional organization and union for elementary and secondary school teachers, counselors, principals, administrators, and college and university professors.

Professional and Trade Periodicals

The Chronicle of Higher Education
1255 23rd St. NW, No. 700
Washington, D.C. 20037
(202) 466-1000
Periodical published 48 times per year reporting trends in higher education.

Education Week
4301 Connecticut Ave. NW
Ste. 250
Washington, DC 20008
(202) 364-4114
Weekly magazine reporting trends in elementary and secondary school education.

The following resources will also keep you updated on industry trends:

Standard & Poor's Industrial Surveys
Standard & Poor's Corp.
25 Broadway
New York, NY 10004
(212) 208-8768
Provides trends, analysis, and projections of approximately 25 major industries. Updated annually but issues more frequent updates on major industry developments.

U.S. Industrial Outlook
U.S. Department of Commerce
Government Printing Office
Washington, D.C. 20402-9325
(202) 783-3238
Annually updates the prospects for over 350 manufacturing and service industries.

Career Trends

The types of career opportunities available at a particular time are directly related to the economic, business, and social trends of that time. Changes in our way of life affect industries, often influencing decline and growth in occupational fields. The child care industry is a good example of this relationship. Women entering and returning to the work force have created a demand for child care services. As a result, there's been a tremendous increase in the number of businesses providing day care, babysitting, preschool programs, and afterschool child care; employment services for nannies and housekeepers; and the training programs for these workers.

In carefully researching and exploring career trends, you'll learn what new jobs are being created, which ones are increasing in number, and which have fewer applicants than openings. The chances of finding employment increases if you pursue a field with greater, rather than diminishing, opportunities.

A research study prepared by the Hudson Institute (see Figure 3) predicts changes in the number of jobs for twenty-five different fields by the year 2000, and shows those occupations it anticipates will see future growth and those that will experience a decline. What are your prime job prospects? According to this forecast, the best opportunities will be in sales, professional, technical, managerial, and service jobs.

Figure 3. The changing occupational structure, 1984–2000.

Occupation	Current Jobs (000s)	New Jobs (000s)	Rate of Growth (Percentage)
Service Occupations	16,059	5,957	37
Managerial and Management Related	10,893	4,280	39
Marketing and Sales	10,656	4,150	39
Administrative Support	18,483	3,620	20
Technicians	3,146	1,389	44
Health Diagnosing and Treating Occupations	2,478	1,384	53
Teachers, Librarians, and Counselors	4,437	1,381	31
Mechanics, Installers, and Repairers	4,264	966	23
Transportation and Heavy Equipment Operators	4,604	752	16
Engineers, Architects, and Surveyors	1,447	600	41
Construction Trades	3,127	595	19
Natural, Computer, and Mathematical Scientists	647	442	68
Writers, Artists, Entertainers, and Athletes	1,092	425	39
Other Professionals and Paraprofessionals	825	355	43
Lawyers and Judges	457	326	71

(continued)

Figure 3 *(continued)*

Occupation	Current Jobs (000s)	New Jobs (000s)	Rate of Growth (Percentage)
Social, Recreational, and Religious Workers	759	235	31
Helpers and Laborers	4,168	205	5
Social Scientists	173	70	40
Precision Production Workers	2,790	61	2
Plant and System Workers	275	36	13
Blue Collar Supervisors	1,442	−6	0
Miners	175	−28	−16
Hand Workers, Assemblers, and Fabricators	2,604	−179	−7
Machine Setters, Operators, and Tenders	5,527	−448	−8
Agriculture, Forestry, and Fisheries	4,480	−538	−12
Total	105,008	25,952	25

Reprinted by permission from Herman Kahn Center, 5395 Emerson Way, *Workforce 2000*, Hudson Institute (Indianapolis, Indiana, 1987, p. 97).

Future Careers

Advances in technology create a bright outlook for new career opportunities. You'll need to research the technology, applications, industry forecasts, and job and career outlooks. The following resource is an excellent start.

New Emerging Careers: Today, Tomorrow, and in the 21st Century
S. Norman Feingold & Maxine H. Atwater
Garrett Park Press
Garrett Park, MD 20896
(301) 946-2553
In-depth guide to future careers in, for example, biotechnology, lasers, robotics, information technology, telecommunications, information management, computers, aerospace, medical technology, and superconductivity. Loaded with resources. 1988.

Portable Careers

Some careers require specific skills that can be performed in almost any industry and allow you the flexibility to move from one industry to another. Although this doesn't always require learning additional skills, it does involve learning another area of business.

This ability to move to other industries is another avenue of continued growth and is a safeguard against becoming stuck in a diminishing industry.

Portable careers include human resources, finance, marketing, customer service, and management.

Human Resources

Some of the positions available in human resources are personnel manager, wage and salary administrator, benefits and compensation manager, labor relations specialist, affirmative action manager, and training and development manager. The following professional associations can provide information on careers in human resources.

Society for Human Resource
    Management
606 N. Washington St.
Alexandria, VA 22314
(703) 548-3440

Employment Management
    Association
5 W. Hargett St., Ste. 1100
Raleigh, NC 27601
(919) 828-6614

American Society of Training and
    Development
Box 1443
1630 Duke St.
Alexandria, VA 22313
(703) 683-8100

Finance

Some of the positions available in finance are accountant, auditor, controller, and credit manager. The following professional associations can provide information on careers in finance.

American Institute of Certified
    Public Accountants
1211 Ave. of the Americas
New York, NY 10036
(212) 575-6200

Institute of Internal Auditors
249 Maitland Ave.
Altamonte Springs, FL 32701-4201
(407) 830-7600

National Association of
    Accountants
Ten Paragon Dr.
Montvale, NJ 07645
(201) 573-9000

National Society of Public
    Accountants
1010 N. Fairfax Street
Alexandria, VA 22314
(703) 549-6400

Financial Executives Institute
Ten Madison Ave.
Box 1938
Morristown, NJ 07960
(201) 898-4600

National Association of Credit
   Management
8815 Centre Park Dr.
Columbia, MD 21045
(301) 740-5560

Marketing

Some of the positions available in marketing are marketing manager, marketing representative, sales manager, and sales representative. The following professional associations can provide information on careers in marketing and sales.

American Marketing Association
250 S. Wacker Dr., Ste. 200
Chicago, IL 60606
(312) 648-0536

Professional Salespersons of
   America
3801 Monaco NE
Albuquerque, NM 87111
(505) 275-0857

Sales & Marketing Executives
   International
Statler Office Tower, #458
Cleveland, OH 44115
(216) 771-6650

Customer Service

One of the positions available in customer service is customer service manager. The following professional association can provide information on careers in customers service.

International Customer Service Association
111 E. Wacker Dr., Ste. 600
Chicago, IL 60601
(312) 644-6610

Management

Some of the positions available in management are executive director, administrator, and manager. The following professional associations can provide information on careers in management.

American Management
   Association
135 W. 50th St.
New York, NY 10020
(212) 586-8100

National Management
   Association
2210 Arbor Blvd.
Dayton, OH 45439
(513) 294-0421

Resources

The following newsletters and periodicals are your best general sources of current and timely career information.

Newsletters

CAM Report
Priam Publications, Inc.
605 Glenmoor, Ste. 2B
Lansing, MI 48823
(517) 351-6093

Published semimonthly, except for one issue each in June, July, August; includes career, industry, and management information.

Career Opportunities News
Garrett Park Press
Garrett Park, MD 20896
(301) 946-2553

Published six times a year, offers a wide range of useful career information and opportunities, resources for free and inexpensive career materials, career shorts, book reviews, minority interests, and resources of special interest to women.

Kennedy Career Strategist
Career Strategies
1153 Wilmette Ave.
Wilmette, IL 60091
(708) 251-1661

Monthly guide to career planning.

Periodicals

Monthly Labor Review
U.S. Department of Labor
Bureau of Labor Statistics
Superintendent of Documents
U.S. Government Printing Office
Washington, DC 20402
(202) 275-3054

Monthly reports on labor projections and career and job outlooks.

Occupational Outlook Quarterly
U.S. Department of Labor
Bureau of Labor Statistics
Superintendent of Documents
U.S. Government Printing Office
Washington, DC 20402
(202) 275-3054

Quarterly publication on career issues and opportunities.

Working Woman
342 Madison Ave.
New York, NY 10173
(212) 309-9800

While geared toward executive, professional, and entrepreneurial women, this magazine's career articles are pertinent to men as well. Covers all career issues including annual salary surveys and the 25 hottest careers.

Chapter 4

Finding Facts

You need lots of information when you build your career. Researching organizations lets you identify the ones you'd like to pursue and helps you prepare for job interviews. In the current dynamic economic environment, you'd also be wise to investigate occupational fields and business and regional stability prior to making work commitments. How will you know what salary to request? The only way to obtain a strong basis for determining and requesting your salary requirements is to research salaries in your field.

There will be many decisions to make; the best decisions are informed decisions, meaning you search for information that enables you to make the best possible choice. You'll have an edge in this process if you can acquire good research skills.

Where to Begin

The library is a great source of information and is the place to begin your research. But all libraries are not the same, even libraries belonging to the same system. Not only do their sizes, budgets, staffs, and services differ but they purchase different periodicals, directories, and materials for their collections.

Regional, large public, and college and university libraries have the most extensive collections, including business and general periodical indexes, business and technical journals, and newspapers.

There are also specialized libraries found at professional and trade associations. Even your local newspaper may have a library open to the public.

The interlibrary loan system allows most libraries throughout the United States to borrow books and articles for you from public, college, university, and other libraries. You supply the specific titles of books and articles you want, and your local library makes the arrangements. As part of the service, materials can also be photocopied for a small fee. Check your library for the maximum number of requests allowed and any fees. The service takes a couple of weeks, so you'll have to use some other means if you're in a hurry.

Many libraries also have access to database systems and will perform searches for you for free or a small fee depending on the complexity of the search.

Identifying Potential Employers

What type of organization do you want to work for? Large or small? For profit or nonprofit? Privately or publicly owned? If in the public sector, do you want to work for the federal, state, or local government? Even when the type of position you are seeking is available in all types of organizations, the jobs may be different because the structure and personality of the organizations differ.

A self-directed job search gives you great flexibility in choosing organizations that meet your needs and values. You can locate these organizations through the directories listed later in this chapter.

Read everything you can about companies and their leaders. Articles in business and trade magazines, journals, newsletters, and newspapers are good sources for identifying senior staff, understanding an organization's philosophy and mission, and learning about its services or products. Soon you'll develop a list of employment possibilities including names, addresses, phone numbers, senior staff, and other information.

Preparing for the Job Interview

Have you done enough research prior to the interview to know how you can fit into the organization? The following ideas will help you thoroughly research an organization prior to the interview.

1. Identify basic information through the directories listed later in this chapter. Learn what the organization does, identify its products and/or services, and find out about its senior staff and officers. You should also know how long the company has been in business, how many subsidiaries it has, its size, and other details.

2. Obtain industry information from professional and trade associations (see Chapters 3 and 6).
3. Use periodical indexes (Chapter 3) to locate articles written about the organization, its senior staff, and its officers. Newspaper articles can also reveal organization and administration personality, mission, goals, and objectives. This information helps you decide whether there's a match between you and the company.
4. Write a background summary of the organization including how long it's been in business, who its competition is, and how it ranks in its industry.
5. It's also a good idea to read up on the industry and to identify trends and projections, as well as problems and predictions regarding, for example, mergers, acquisitions, pending litigation, and bankruptcies.

Use this information to develop as well as answer questions. For example:

> "I read in *The Wall Street Journal* that you're planning to merge with ABC Company. How does the marketing department fit in to this new structure?"
>
> "Will you be developing a new long-distance service now that MCI has introduced one?"
>
> "What direction do you see your organization going in if the government passes the new bill on construction restrictions?"

Make sure you can confidently answer the question, "What do you know about our company?" Prepare to intersperse information that you've gathered to support the answers to your questions.

Research Ideas

Be resourceful, creative, and actively pursue information. Your time and effort will pay off in useful facts. Use the following ideas to research publicly and privately held companies and organizations in the private sector.

Private Sector

Companies that are publicly held (owned by stockholders) are often easier to research than privately held companies (not listed on any stock exchange). By law, publicly held companies must make certain types of information available to their stockholders and the public.

Contact the company public relations department and request that an annual report (only available if it's publicly held) and any brochures, in-house newsletters, magazines, or promotional materials be sent to you by first-class mail. Or you can arrange to pick them up. Other places to look for annual reports and corporate literature are in college, university, and high school career centers. Also try your local, college, and university libraries. Finally, a corporation's own historian or information library may be able to supply additional information.

Identify the corporate officers and top management through corporate directories. Use periodical indexes to locate articles by or about the company, its management, and industry. Obtain copies of these articles.

Use your contacts to locate current or past employees. They can supply firsthand information about the organization's dynamics.

Rose K., a recent job hunter, explains how prior research can really help:

> I wanted to make a change from a county government to a trade association and after sending letters and making numerous phone calls, I lined up an interview for a job I really wanted in a local trade association.
>
> Prior to the interview, I went to the public library to do some research. I checked in a business periodical index and found several articles about the association. My library had back copies of the periodicals and I made photocopies of the articles.
>
> One of the articles was written by the individual who was going to interview me. While I read all of the articles carefully, made notes, and developed a few questions, I paid particular attention to the article written by the interviewer. I highlighted all of his buzz words and made notes of his philosophy.
>
> On the day of the interview I decided to wear a red suit instead of my traditional navy blue because I had gotten the impression from the article that the interviewer was a flashy kind of guy. The interview went extremely well. I incorporated many of the highlighted buzz words and the interviewer's philosophy in my answers.
>
> I got the job and on my first day of work my new boss, the interviewer, approached me and after we finished talking he said, "Oh, by the way, I just loved your red suit!"

The following books, directories, and newsletters will help you research companies. A complete list of periodical indexes is located in Chapter 3.

Books

Business Information Sources
Lorna M. Daniells
University of California Press
2120 Berkeley Way
Berkeley, CA 94720
(415) 642-4247
Provides extensive information on locating facts, including information on companies, organizations, and individuals. 1985.

How to Find Information About Companies: The Corporate Intelligence Source Book
Washington Researchers Publishing
2612 P St. NW
Washington, DC 20007
(202) 333-3533
Guide to thousands of company information sources for researching public, private, domestic, or foreign companies.

Corporate Directories

America's Corporate Families
Dun's Marketing Services, Inc.
Three Sylvan Way
Parsippany, NJ 07054
(800) 526-0651
Includes 500 parent companies with annual sales of $1 billion or more. There are 11,000 ultimate parent companies and over 55,000 subsidiary companies and divisions owned by these ultimate parent companies. Annually updated.

Directory of Corporate Affiliations
National Register Publishing Co.
3004 Glenview Rd.
Wilmette, IL 60091
(708) 441-2210; (800) 323-6772
In-depth view of major U.S. corporations and their divisions, subsidiaries, affiliates. Provides information on "who owns whom." Cross-references over 40,000 divisions, subsidiaries, and affiliates with parent companies. Lists information on over 4,000 parent companies and includes geographical index. Annually updated.

Directory of Foreign Firms Operating in the United States
Uniworld Business Publications, Inc.
50 E. 42nd St.
New York, NY 10017
Includes approximately 1,600 foreign firms in 50 countries and more than 2,500 businesses in the United States which are wholly or partly owned by them. Lists phone numbers, types of businesses, chief officers, and number of employees.

International Directory of Corporate Affiliations
National Register Publishing Co.
3004 Glenview Rd.
Wilmette, IL 60091
(708) 441-2210; (800) 323-6772
In-depth view of major multinational companies, subsidiaries, and affiliates. Provides information on "who owns whom." Cross-references over 30,000 divisions, subsidiaries, and affiliates with parent company. Lists information on

over 1,600 foreign parent companies. Includes geographical index. Annually updated.

MacMillan Directory of Leading Private Companies
National Register Publishing Co.
3004 Glenview Rd.
Wilmette, IL 60091
(708) 441-2210; (800) 323-6772

Provides information on approximately 10,000 companies and wholly owned subsidiaries in the United States. Includes addresses, phone numbers, some financial information, officers' names, computer systems and hardware, outside service firms, and names of wholly owned subsidiaries. Annually updated.

Million Dollar Directory
Dun's Marketing Services, Inc.
Three Sylvan Way
Parsippany, NJ 07054
(800) 526-0651

Includes information on 160,000 U.S. businesses with a net worth of over $500,000. More than 140,000 listings of privately owned businesses. Headquarter addresses, phone numbers, annual sales volumes, number of employees, and names of corporate officers and boards of directors. Annually updated.

Moody's Industrial Manual
Moody's Investor Service
99 Church St.
New York, NY 10007
(212) 553-0300

Includes information on companies on the New York and American Stock Exchanges, their lines of business, major officers, and financial information. Annually updated; biweekly supplements.

Standard Corporate Descriptions
Standard & Poor's Corporation
25 Broadway
New York, NY 10004
(212) 208-8702

Descriptions of various publicly held corporations (companies pay a fee to be listed). Includes capitalization backgrounds, unit data, stock data, earnings, and finances. Published semimonthly.

Standard & Poor's Register of Corporations
Standard & Poor's Corporation
[see above]

Volume I: Corporate listings for 55,000 corporations. Includes addresses, phone numbers, titles, and functions of approximately 450,000 officers and directors, descriptions of companys' products/service, annual sales, number of employees, division names and functions, and subsidiary listings. Annually updated.

Volume II: Over 70,000 individuals serving as officers, directors, trustees, and partners. Principal business affiliations with official titles, business addresses, residence addresses, year and place of birth (where obtainable), college and year of graduation, fraternal memberships.

Volume III: Cross-referenced index lists subsidiaries, divisions, and affiliates in alphabetical sequence.

Thomas Register
Thomas Publishing Company
One Penn Plaza
New York, NY 10001
(212) 695-0500

Twelve-volume set with a company profiles section that lists more than 145,000 U.S. companies including: corporate addresses, phone numbers, asset ratings, company executives, locations of sales offices, plants, and some subsidiary/division and product line information. Annually updated.

Ward's Business Directory of U.S.
  Private and Public Companies
Information Access Company
362 Lakeside Dr.
Foster City, CA 94404
(800) 227-8431
Company profiles, descriptions, financial data, and market share information
for 85,000 private and public companies. Includes alphabetical and geographical listings. Annually updated.

General Directories

Directories in Print
Julie E. Towell &
  Charles B. Montrey, Eds.
Gale Research Company
835 Penobscot Bldg.
Detroit, MI 48226
(313) 961-2242; (800) 347-GALE

Guide to approximately 10,000 business and industrial directories, professional and scientific rosters, and
directory databases.

National Directory of Magazines
Oxbridge Communications, Inc.
150 Fifth Ave., Ste. 636
New York, NY 10011
(212) 741-0231
Comprehensive guide to large and small
U.S. and Canadian magazines

Oxbridge Directory of
  Newsletters
Oxbridge Communications, Inc.
[*see above*]
Claims to be the most comprehensive
guide to U.S. and Canadian newsletters.

Regional Directories

Most states publish an industrial directory, and many counties publish
a business and industry directory through their economic development
authority. Regional directories are found in the reference section of
your public library.

Specialized Industry Directories

There are hundreds of directories for special industries. For example, if
you're interested in working in a library, you could consult *American
Library Directory* by R. R. Bowker. The Directory lists public, academic,
government, and special libraries in the United States and Canada and
includes names, addresses, phone numbers, key personnel, income
and expenditures (including salaries), special subjects, and collections.

Locate industry directories in *Directories in Print*, listed in the
previous section of this chapter, or check with the reference librarian at
your public library.

Newsletters

Corporate Jobs Outlook!
Drawer 100
Boerne, TX 78006-0100
(512) 755-8810; (800) 325-8808

Bimonthly newsletter containing reports on 16 or 17 major companies with 5,000 or more employees and offices through out the United States. Totals 100 reports per year. Includes information on salaries and benefits, current and projected developments, suggested reading lists, and additional inside information. Back issues available.

Public Sector

While researching the public sector may require a little imagination, it's just as important to identify issues and key players in these organizations.

Budgets for federal, state, county, city, town, and village governments are a matter of public record and are available for review in public libraries and government offices.

Most public organizations produce in-house newsletters. Request copies as well as any other published literature through their public affairs office. Contact the Office of Public Liaison at any federal government agencies to see if they can send you fact sheets, which might include mission, history, authority, budget, type of work, programs, and additional activities.

Scan local newspapers and periodicals for articles on issues, budgets, board members, politicians, and government officials. Check periodical indexes for articles about the organization and its top management.

County and city governments often publish handbooks and profiles including extensive demographic information. Check the Office of Research and Statistics or visit your local public library. Both usually keep copies of all published documents from local government. Even telephone directories sometimes include short histories and information about local government. Many public libraries also have phone directories from all over the United States.

The following resources will help you research organizations in the public sector.

Federal Government

Computer Software

Federal Occupational and Career Information System (FOCIS)
NTIS
5285 Port Royal Rd.
Springfield, VA 22161
(703) 487-4650

Program for IBM PC or compatible. Alphabetical listing of agencies by subdivision, regions, states, and cities providing agency descriptions and addresses. Requires a high-density (1.2 megabyte) 5¼-inch disk drive. For more information about program, see Chapter 2.

Directories

Federal Career Directory
Office of Personnel Management
U.S. Government Printing Office
Washington, DC 20402
(202) 783-3238
Comprehensive information and profiles on agencies and their departments, job opportunities, required degrees, and resources for further information. In-

cludes information on benefits, training and development opportunities, the federal pay system, the personnel classification system, and how to apply for federal employment. 1990.

U.S. Government Manual
Office of Federal Register
U.S. Government Printing Office
Washington, DC 20402
(202) 783-3238
Contains comprehensive information on federal agencies in the judicial, legislative, and executive branches. Lists summary statement of agency's purpose, principal officials, and agency history as well as descriptions of programs and activities. Indexed by name of agency, subject, and recent changes. 1989/1990.

State/Local Government

Directories

Moody's Municipal and Government Manual
Moody's Investor Service
99 Church St.
New York, NY 10007
(212) 553-0300
Provides demographic, economic, and financial information on states and municipalities. Annually updated.

Databases

With a personal computer, a modem, and communications software, your research options increase: You can access on-line databases to research any business topic; get business news from *The Wall Street Journal* and major wire services; access periodical indexes, directories, and actual articles; review current financial data; identify recent management changes; discover new products; and obtain lists of executives.

Using a large on-line database requires technical expertise and research experience. Also, conducting a search is expensive, since you pay a membership fee as well as for connect time. As an alternative, try an online information service for the nontechnical user—for example, CompuServe, PC-LINK, GEnie, or DELPHI. These services are widely available and much cheaper.

If you lack technical skills and have no access to an on-line information service, it may be more cost-efficient to have an on-line database search conducted by a professional researcher. This can be done through your local library or an information broker. For a listing of information brokers check:

*Directory of Fee-Based
   Information Services*
Burwell Enterprises
3724 FM1960 W., Ste. 214
Houston, TX 77068
(713) 537-9051

Listing of 1,000 companies and individuals providing information services for a fee. Indexes listings by subject area, services, and city. Annually updated.

Directories for Locating
   Databases

*Datapro Directory of
   On-Line Services*
Datapro Research Corporation
1805 Underwood Blvd.
Delran, NJ 08075
(609) 764-0100; (800) 257-9406
Includes databases, producers, and on-line services.

Directory of Online Databases
Cuadra/Elsevier
Box 872
Madison Square Garden
New York, NY 10159
(212) 989-5800
Lists over 4,000 databases.

*Computer-Based
   Services Directory*
Telenet Communications
   Corporation

Attn: Telemarketing, HQ14 E.
   12490 Sunrise Valley Dr.
Reston, VA 22096
(703) 689-5700; (800) 835-3638
Lists hundreds of commercial databases.

The Leading On-Line
   Databases

*Dow Jones News/Retrieval
   Information Services Group*
Dow Jones & Company, Inc.
Box 300
Princeton, NJ 08543-0300
(609) 520-4649
Over 35 business news- and analysis-oriented databases.

Knowledge Index
Dialog Information Services, Inc.
3460 Hillview Ave.
Palo Alto, CA 94304
(800) 334-2564
An after-hours service that allows you to access 80 popular databases. Reduced rates.

The Leading On-Line
   Information Services
CompuServe
CompuServe Information Service,
   Inc.
5000 Arlington Centre Blvd.
Columbus, OH 43220
(617) 457-8600; (800) 848-8990

DELPHI
General Videotex Corporation
3 Blackstone St.
Cambridge, MA 02139
(617) 491-3393; (800) 544-4005

GEnie
401 N. Washington St.
Rockville, MD 20850
(800) 638-9636

PC-LINK
Quantum Computer Services, Inc.
8619 Westwood Center Dr.
Vienna, VA 22182
(703) 448-8700; (800) 458-8532

Fax Service

If you need facts fast but don't have access to a database, you can have the most current news and extensive background information on thousands of publicly traded companies delivered to your fax machine or via electronic mail. For information contact:

FACTS DELIVERED
Dow Jones Information Services
1-800-445-9454, weekdays from 9 A.M. to 6 P.M. EST

Salaries

Most jobs have salary ranges—starting, mid-point, and maximum. A particular job may have several salary ranges, depending on whether the position is entry- or senior-level. You must know the range of salary and what your skills, experience, training, and education are worth in the workplace.

Fortunately, annual salary surveys are conducted by professional and trade associations, employment agencies, executive search firms, outplacement firms, trade publications, and periodicals. *Working Woman* magazine, for example, publishes an annual survey every January. Robert Half International, Inc., publishes an annual salary survey for accounting, finance, and information systems jobs. These types of organizations and periodicals can be located through directories.

Your state employment commission or the placement office at your local college, university, or professional and trade school can tell you what the current salary is in your career field at your education and experience level.

Be direct and call the organization with the job opening. Request the salary range for the position.

Job advertisements in current issues of the *National Business Employment Weekly*, a national publication advertising jobs from all occupations, will give you an idea of current salaries.

Individuals currently holding the type of position you seek may be willing to share the salary range with you.

The following books are good sources of salary information.

The American Almanac of
  Jobs and Salaries
John W. Wright &
  Edward J. Dwyer
Avon Books
105 Madison Ave.
New York, NY 10016
(212) 481-5653

Excellent, valuable source book on the U.S. job market together with salaries. Background information on specific careers. Covers federal, local, and state governments, the postal service, and the private sector. 1990.

Occupational Outlook Handbook
U.S. Department of Labor
Bureau of Labor Statistics
U.S. Government Printing Office
Washington, DC 20402

Provides average salaries and salary ranges. Updated every other year. 1990.

Professional Careers Sourcebook
Kathleen M. Savage &
  Charity Anne Dorgan, Eds.
Gale Research, Inc.
835 Penobscot Bldg.
Detroit, MI 48226-4094
(313) 961-2242; (800) 347-GALE

Includes salary ranges for 111 careers requiring college degrees or specialized education. 1990.

Chapter 5

Building a Skill

Will you successfully find and keep employment in the 1990s? The answer to this question depends on your willingness to acquire skills that keep pace with changes in both technology and the workplace, and on your commitment to lifelong learning.

How can you prepare for the future when you don't know for sure what it will be like? You can meet the challenges and changes ahead by developing a willingness to learn. Be open to change, and consider the possibility that what you have been doing may be done differently and more effectively some other way.

Whatever your formal education, training, or certification, your education will never be complete. It will be supplemented and updated with a lifelong endeavor of continuing education.

> Someone once said, "You can't teach an old dog new tricks." That concept sticks in a lot of people's minds and it has nothing to do with human learning. Human beings can learn at any point in their lives and careers. They may learn differently and at a different pace or rate, but they do learn.
>
> Ken Plum,
> Director of Adult Education,
> Fairfax County Public Schools

A wide variety of learning methods are available to help you integrate this process into your schedule and meet your learning preferences too. Do you learn best by reading or must you hear something to understand it? Do you like working independently or working in a group and sharing and hearing other people's experiences? You can do it on your own with books, workbooks, audiotapes, and computer software or learn from others in a classroom setting that structures your time and creates the framework for learning.

If you shouted with glee when you completed your formal education, you may be resistant to the idea of not only learning more, but learning forever. What we're really talking about is gaining knowledge and understanding and you'll do this not just by studying, but by experiencing. You won't learn strictly by rote or memorization, but by doing and practicing.

You might want to begin this adventure by sharpening your learning skills. The following books, tapes, and self-study programs will make the task easier and more pleasurable by strengthening and improving your reading, listening, and retaining skills.

Audiocassette Programs

How to Improve Your Memory
American Management
    Association
Extension Institute
Box 1026
Saranac Lake, NY 12983-9986
(518) 891-5510

An audiocassette workbook program, including six cassettes and workbook with quizzes and exercises, designed to increase your learning and listening by expanding your capacity to memorize and recall. Includes basic learning principles and numerous memory techniques. Course service staff available to grade quizzes and provide feedback. One Continuing Education Unit (CEU) available upon completion.

Memory Power
CareerTrack
3085 Center Green Dr.
Boulder, CO 80301-5408
(303) 442-0392; (800) 334-1018

Includes four audiocassettes offering techniques and special applications helping you learn and remember including reading and hearing recall, learning a foreign language, and increasing your memory and energy with nutrition.

Books

More Learning in Less Time
Norma B. Kahn
Ten Speed Press
Box 7123
Berkeley, CA 94707
(415) 845-8414

Wonderful, easy to read book that will improve your reading, listening, note taking, writing, and retention. Helpful tips and strategies, clearly written and well organized, that will make you a better learner. 1989.

Self-Study Programs

*Reading Power: Getting the Most
    From What You Read*
American Management
    Association
Extension Institute
Box 1026
Saranac Lake, NY 12983-9986
(518) 891-5510

Self-paced study program to help you double your reading speed, improve your accuracy, and build on your comprehension. Pretest, self-diagnostic tests, course service staff support, objective test, and case study. Earn two CEUs.

You may be shying away from the stock market these days, but here's one hot tip that will pay off for years to come: Build and update your skills. There's a current shortage of highly skilled employees, and they're being referred to as gold-collar workers—*gold* meaning *cash* because the pool of highly skilled workers is shrinking and employers think that these men and women will soon be able to name their own salaries. Doesn't that sound appealing?

But while employers are feeling a shortage of gold-collar workers, they aren't interested in investing money in training; rather, they are seeking individuals who have skills, are good learners, and can use their skills for future growth.

Acquiring a skill takes discipline, motivation, and time. Skills aren't developed simply by reading or attending workshops. You have to study, apply the information, and practice, practice, practice!

If you want a competitive edge in the job market, acquire marketable skills. Labor market and human resources experts cite the following as the eight most desirable skills:

1. Computer literacy
2. Creativity
3. Foreign language
4. Leadership
5. Math
6. Problem solving
7. Speaking
8. Writing

Increase your marketability by combining several skills, such as math and a foreign language, or writing and computer knowledge.

Opportunities to learn are everywhere. Self-help books, tapes, videos, and computer software easily fit into busy life-styles and allow you to learn independently and at your own pace. A multitude or workshops are offered through adult education and continuing education programs sponsored by local public schools, community colleges, and universities, as well as by private schools and programs and community and nonprofit organizations. Workshops provide information, motivation, and the opportunity to practice and sharpen your skills.

The following section gives you information on how to acquire, or sharpen, any or all of these eight skills. There's a description of the skill, a list of activities to help you develop it, and recommended resources (for example, reading materials and audio and videotapes) to develop and reinforce your learning.

Computer Literacy

We live in an information age, and the person with access to the information has the power. Computer technology provides significant benefits, from saving time and providing information, to creating efficiency in handling paperwork. An asset on your current job, computer knowledge opens doors to new and future career options.

While you won't need to know how to write a computer program, if you are to compete in the workplace, you'll need to be skilled in basic personal computer (PC) operations, as well as in using applications software.

The personal computer is a tool that can amplify a certain part of our inherent intelligence.

Steven Jobs,
Cofounder,
Apple Computer Company

Begin by deciding whether you want to use the IBM PC or the Macintosh. While the Macintosh is easier to learn and use, the IBM has more business applications and is generally recognized as a "business" computer. However, new business programs are becoming available for the Macintosh, so base your choice on your intended business environment.

Employers seek expertise with both word processing and spreadsheet programs. Knowledge of a database program is a plus. Determine your business/career needs and learn the appropriate applications.

Activities

If you know how to type or use a keyboard, you're in good shape. If not, you'll need to get familiar with the keyboard, either in a workshop or with a software program.

Get comfortable with the computer in an introduction to the computer class. Learn how the computer operates and take the opportunity to practice. Check within your present organization to see if computer training is available. If not, there are workshops at computer retail stores, private companies, and adult and continuing education programs.

Develop computer expertise by learning software programs and working with them regularly. Do you have a computer at work? If so, make learning the computer your first priority. If you don't, consider purchasing your own. Additional options are renting or leasing a computer or renting computer time in a computer lab through adult and continuing education programs or computer stores.

Join a users group. Users groups unite individuals with a common interest and provide information, resources, and support. Locate users groups through your local computer store, internally within your organization, and in the business section of your local newspaper and local computer periodicals.

Subscribe to computer magazines to keep current on products, trends, and applications. Choose from the following magazines:

Home Office Computing
Scholastic, Inc.
730 Broadway
New York, NY 10003
(800) 365-2270
While targeting to individuals interested in entrepreneurship, this monthly magazine also offers excellent reviews on software and products.

MacWorld
MacWorld Communication, Inc.
501 Second St., Ste. 600
San Francisco, CA 94107
(415) 243-0505
Monthly magazine for Macintosh users.

MacUser
Box 56986
Boulder, CO 80321
(800) 525-0643; (303) 447-9330
Monthly magazine for Macintosh users.

PC/Computing
Four Cambridge Center
Cambridge, MA 02142
(800) 365-2270

Monthly magazine for IBM PC users that features reviews on software and products plus helpful information on how to effectively use your computer.

PC Novice
Peed Corp.
120 W. Harvest Dr.
Lincoln, NE 68521
(800) 848-1478
Monthly magazine for IBM PC users that is filled with helpful information for the beginning computer user.

PC World
PC World Communications, Inc.
501 Second St.
San Francisco, CA 94107
(800) 234-3498
Monthly magazine for IBM PC users that is geared toward computer business applications.

Decide which applications and software programs you'll master. A wide variety of learning methods are available to suit your needs from books, software, and audiocassettes to videos. Publishers for these types of resources are listed below.

Books

Bantam Computer Books
666 Fifth Ave.
New York, NY 10103-0023
(800) 223-5780
Catalog of books on PCs, word processing, spreadsheets, database management, desktop publishing, on-line services, and Macintosh.

Compute!
Chilton Book Co.
One Chilton Way
Radnor, PA 19089
(215) 964-4000; (800) 345-1214
Catalog of books on business applications for IBM PC and compatibles and Macintosh computers. Offers a Quick Start and Easy Reference Series for database, graphics, word processing, spreadsheet, and desktop publishing software.

TAB Books
Blue Ridge Summit, PA 17294-0850
(800) 822-8138
Catalog of books on business software for Apple computers and business software for IBM computers.

Que
11711 N. College Ave.
Box 90
Carmel, IN 46032
(317) 573-2510; (800) 428-5331
Catalog of books on business software for Macintosh computers and business software for IBM computers.

SYBEX, Inc.
2021 Challenger Dr., #100
Alameda, CA 94501
(800) 227-2346
Catalog of books on Apple, Macintosh, IBM PC, computer literacy, database management, desktop presentation and publishing, operating systems, word processing, and more.

Disks, Videotapes, and Audiocassette Programs

American Training International (ATI)
12638 Beatrice St.
Los Angeles, CA 90066
(213) 823-1129; (800) 421-4827
Skill-based training using disks. Carries a broad range of training disks for popular software programs including: introduction to your computer, operating systems, word processing, integrated software, database management, spreadsheets, and specialized software programs. Video-based training also available.

Anderson Soft-Teach
2680 N. First St.
San Jose, CA 95134
(408) 434-0100
Video-based training programs include practice disks for computer literacy, MS/PC DOS, Lotus 1-2-3 releases, WordPerfect, Microsoft Word, Displaywrite, dBase IV, Symphony, and Lotus Agenda.

FlipTrack Learning Systems
999 Main St., Dept. 990
Glen Ellyn, IL 60137
(800) 222-FLIP
Over forty computer and software courses including audiocassettes, diskette, and guide.

Individual Software Inc.
125 Shoreway Rd., Ste. 3000
San Carlos, CA 94070-2704
(415) 595-8855
Software tutorials: Learn to TYPE, Learn to Use DOS, Learn To Use Your PC, and additional IBM PC software programs.

MacAcademy
477 S. Nova Rd.
Ormond Beach, FL 32174
(800) 527-1914
Over forty different training videos for Macintosh computer programs.

VideoTutor
110 Wild Basin Rd., Ste. 280
Austin, TX 78746
(512) 328-3721; (800) 252-1255
Software tutorials for the most popular programs for IBM PC and Macintosh computers. Includes videotape, workbook, and exercise diskette.

Creativity

Do you equate the word *creativity* with childhood, crayons, and finger paint? If so, you've probably found yourself caught in a web of "sameness." Sticking to routine and procedures can lead to dreary, predictable results, while creativity fosters innovative ideas, unique methods and solutions, and productive outcomes.

The majority of new ideas are not unusual; what is unusual is the experience of having new ideas.

Anonymous

Creativity has no age restrictions. It draws on your imagination and intuition to produce enhanced performance, increased productivity, and goal realization.

Original thinking and ideas are within your reach. Creativity can be applied to business situations enabling you to solve problems, plan effectively, and develop innovative ideas and solutions.

Activities

The following activities are designed to spark your creative juices and develop fresh ideas.

• *Change your environment.* If it's noisy, go someplace quiet; if it's quiet, go someplace noisy. Getting out in the fresh air often clears your mind and gets the ideas flowing.

• *Concentrate on an entirely different activity.* Go for a walk, ride your bike, bake a cake, wash the car, whatever you'd like that relaxes you.

• *Listen to music: classical, rock, folk, whatever.* Words are stimulating while music often plays into your memory and association.

• *Develop brainstorming techniques.* Find your own system of generating, organizing, and fleshing out ideas.

It's time to arouse your resourcefulness, cleverness, and curiosity. The following resources are filled with techniques to improve your creativity.

Resources

In addition to the following, see the entry for The Center for Creative Leadership under *Leadership* later in this chapter.

Audiocassette Programs

Pocket Innovator
American Management
  Association
Extension Institute
Box 1026
Saranac Lake, NY 12983-9986
(518) 891-5510

A seven-stage creative development process including a compact deck of plastic cards, user's guide, and audio-cassette designed to help you generate innovative ideas and solutions.

Books

A Kick in the Seat of the Pants
Roger von Oech
Harper & Row Publishers, Inc.
10 E. 53rd St.
New York, NY 10022
(212) 207-7000

Highly recommended book identifies the four roles of the creative process and provides numerous exercises to bring out your creativity. Humorous approach and loaded with visuals. 1986.

Cards

The Creative Whack Pack
Roger von Oech
Warner Books, Inc.
666 Fifth Ave.
New York, NY 10103
(212) 484-2900; (800) 638-6460

Pack of 64 cards designed to spark creativity through lively anecdotes, slogans, and illustrations. 1990.

Videos

Tapping Into Your Creativity
American Management Association
Video Customer Service Center
Nine Galen St.
Box 9119
Watertown, MA 02272-9901
(617) 926-4600; (800) 225-3215
Techniques, insights, and simple devices enabling you to draw out your imagination, humor, intuition, playfulness and apply them to real-life situations.

Foreign Language

The world is shrinking. International commerce has increased, expanding business opportunities in Latin America, the Pacific Rim, and Eastern Europe. The United States has become more and more interdependent and dependent on other countries. You can benefit from these changes and opportunities by learning to communicate in a foreign language.

Times have changed. In the past, people from countries who wanted to do business with the United States learned English just to do business with us. Because English was used for international commerce, we Americans became very spoiled. We live in a big country with a homogeneous language, and our neighbor up north just happens to speak it too. But many of our European counterparts, who live next door to countries having a different language, are fluent in five or six.

Learning a foreign language not only opens the door to job possibilities but enhances an existing career and makes learning a second foreign language easier. It also teaches you more about your own language in the process.

Which language you choose to learn depends on how this skill will benefit your job and work environment. Spanish is the most needed language; Japanese is growing in demand, followed by, in no particular order, French, German, Portuguese, Italian, Japanese, and Chinese. Your goal is to speak the language easily and develop a fluency. You don't need to speak like a native, but you do need to communicate. Technical, commercial, and slang vocabulary may be needed in your work environment as well.

Some people seem to have a special ability, a "knack," for learning languages. If you're not one of these souls, language fluency is still within your reach; you'll just have to work harder and allow more time to achieve your goal. Learning a language requires self-discipline and different learning skills. For this reason, it's often easier to make progress in a formalized, structured classroom approach.

You'll find learning opportunities from audiotapes to classes and private tutors. All three have a place in learning languages. A teacher or tutor provides constructive feedback as well as allowing you to see facial and body expressions, such as how to hold your hands and mouth. An audiotape allows repetitive hearing for practice and reinforcement.

Activities

Select audiotapes carefully and use them regularly as a supplement to a structured program. Some audiotapes are completely in a foreign language while others alternate with your language. You'll find tapes that are conversational—developed for travel, not fluency—while others are developed as companions to textbooks. Ask your teacher or tutor for recommendations.

Learn in frequent, short sessions. You'll retain more, make progress, and be encouraged to learn more. Language should be functional; if what you're leaning is useful, you'll remember it.

Immerse yourself in the language by visiting the target country or accepting a foreign exchange student or a live-in housekeeper. Look for someone in the work place fluent in the language and ask that person to converse with you only in that language. Use your imagination to find and interact with native speakers. Locate them through a local university or church, religious groups, or a native grocery store from the targeted country.

When you've progressed to advanced beginner status, plan and seek out opportunities to practice in real-life situations. Order magazine and newspaper subscriptions in the foreign language to supplement your reading of books. Attend films and meet and converse with others fluent in that language.

Most important, don't give up. Learning a foreign language is a highly desirable credential.

The following resources will help you prepare to reach your goals.

Audiocassette Programs

Pimsleur Language Programs
American Management Association
Extension Institute
Box 1026
Saranac Lake, NY 12983-9986
(518) 891-5510

Self-instructive language program that guarantees you'll reach a conversational level in thirty days if you use the tapes one half hour every day. Includes fifteen to sixteen audiocassettes and a study guide. Available in Spanish, French, German, Russian, and Italian.

Additional audiocassettes are listed under *Foreign Language Instruction* in:

On Cassette
R. R. Bowker
245 W. 17th St.
New York, NY 10011
(800) 346-6049
A comprehensive bibliography of spoken word audiocassettes, listing over 38,000 titles from over 800 producers.

Books

How to Learn a Foreign Language
Graham E. Fuller
Storm King Press
1025 Thomas Jefferson St. NW, Ste. 400—E Lobby
Washington, DC 20007
(202) 944-4224
Excellent book providing an overview of what it takes to learn a foreign language. Encouraging, uplifting, filled with support and ideas to be used as a companion guide to formal language study, as well as suggestions on how to go it alone. 1987.

Leadership

Middle-management positions continue to decline and many managers face a slowdown in upward mobility. As we move on through the decade, there will be stiffer competition for promotions and senior-level positions.

If you plan to compete effectively for management opportunities, you'll have to acquire leadership skills. The first step in the process is understanding what differentiates leaders from managers. Managers monitor staff while leaders motivate, persuade, influence, and inspire others. In *If I'm in Charge, Why Is Everybody Laughing?* David Campbell defines a leader's role as, "motivating, directing, assigning tasks, assessing performance, inspiring by example, coaching, following up."[1] What truly differentiates managers from leaders? Superior people skills.

---

1. David Campbell, *If I'm in Charge, Why Is Everybody Laughing?* (Greensboro, NC: Center for Creative Leadership, 1984), p. 68.

> Leadership is a manager's ability to get subordinates to develop their capabilities by inspiring them to achieve.
>
> John A. Reinecke and William F. Schoell,
> *Introduction to Business*

Activities

Leaders are effective communicators who share their expectations with their staffs and others. Follow the activities listed under speaking and writing skills.

Read and use books, audiocassettes, and self-study programs for ideas and inspiration, making notes on effective techniques, and begin applying and integrating the information and approaches into your work.

Find role models in your organization or industry. Watch others carefully and model your behavior after leaders you feel have good leadership skills.

Attend hands-on workshops where there's role playing and the opportunity to practice ideas and techniques.

Use assessment instruments, such as the Myers-Briggs Type Indicator (MBTI). This instrument (explained in Chapter 2) provides information on your personality type. The information enables you to understand yourself and how you can work more effectively with others. The following resource ties the MBTI into effectively improving and enhancing your leadership skills:

The Leadership Equation
Barr & Barr
Eakin Press
Box 23069
Austin, TX 78735
Excellent resource providing information on how to deal effectively with all of the personality types referenced in the MBTI. 1989.

Additional resources provide workable and practical information.

(*continues*)

Audiocassette Programs

How to Get Results With People
Jeff Salzman
CareerTrack
3085 Center Green Dr.
Boulder, CO 80301-5408
(303) 440-7440; (800) 334-1018
An audiocassette program including four cassettes to help build leadership skills. Includes information on building strong relationships, power and leadership, motivating for results, persuasion and negotiation, and developing rapport.

Leadership Training
  CareerTrack
Lou Heckler
[*see above*]
An audiocassette program including four cassettes outlining the qualities of leadership and step-by-step techniques to acquire them.

Books

If I'm in Charge Here Why Is Everybody Laughing?
David Campbell
The Center for Creative Leadership
Box 26300
Greensboro, NC 27402
(919) 288-3999
You'll find out that leadership is demanding, enriching, and exhilarating in an easy to read and humorous format. Provides roles and characteristics of leadership with tips on how to obtain them. 1984.

Leadership
James MacGregor Burns
Harper & Row Publishers, Inc.
Ten E. 53rd St.
New York, NY 10022
(212) 207-7000

This book is a classic, providing a thorough, historical approach to leadership. 1978.

Organizations

The Center for Creative Leadership
Box P-1
Greensboro, NC 27402-1660
(919) 545-2810
A nonprofit educational institution whose mission is developing and encouraging effective management and creative leadership, offers a few quarterly publication, *Issues & Observations*, and a resource guide of effective books, reports, audio and videotapes and instruments on the topics of leadership and creativity.

Self-Study Programs

Leadership Skills for Executives
American Management Association
Extension Institute
Box 1026
Saranac Lake, NY 12983-9986
(518) 891-5510
Self-paced study program highlights the differences between managers and leaders, outlining the skills you'll need to become a successful leader. Course service-staff support, objective test, and case study. Earn two Continuing Education Units (CEUs).

Videos

High Impact Leadership
Mark Sanborn
CareerTrack
[*see above*]
Two-volume video seminar (can be purchased separately) highlighting the differences between managers and leaders and detailing how you can maximize your potential and become a leader.

Math

Don't miss out on career and promotional opportunities because of math intimidation, anxiety, and avoidance. If you're like many others, you may be avoiding work responsibilities and activities that deal with numbers.

Anyone can learn and use basic math. Only individuals progressing to advanced mathematics need a mathematical ability.

> It can be very painful to discover mid-career... that we cannot get facts from our figures or that an occupation that looked comfortably free of mathematics at the lower levels will require familiarity with quantitative methods for advancement.
>
> Sheila Tobias,
> *Overcoming Math Anxiety*

Activities

Get comfortable with math through readings on math history and the science of numbers.

Learn different reading habits. Important points aren't reinforced throughout a chapter, but stated just once. Avoid skimming, and read thoroughly.

Practice and improve conceptual skills, and thinking in order, with math games, such as the Rubik's Cube.

Do word problems and math puzzles. Sheila Tobias, in *Overcoming Math Anxiety*, suggests you do word problems every day. Her book, recommended below, provides numerous problems, strategies for resolving them, and answers.

Seek help at math clinics in adult and continuing education programs sponsored by public school systems, colleges, and universities.

(continues)

Aids

Math Products Plus
Box 64
San Carlos, CA 94070
(415) 593-2839
Extensive catalog of math resource, reference, and enrichment books, math puzzles, math history and diversion books, and math calendars.

Janson Publications, Inc.
222 Richmond St., Ste. 105
Providence, RI 02903
(401) 272-0009; (800) 322-MATH
Extensive catalog of math puzzle, problem, and resource books.

Books

The Little Black Book of
  Business Math
Michael C. Thomsett
AMACOM Books
135 W. 50th St.
New York, NY 10020
(212) 586-8100
Filled with information, exercises, and answers for all types of business math. 1988.

Overcoming Math Anxiety
Sheila Tobias
Houghton Mifflin Co.
Two Park St.
Boston, MA 02108
(617) 725-5000
Excellent book filled with ideas and support in improving math skills. Includes examples, diagrams, explanations on how to use fractions, the many meanings of minus, averages and averaging, and calculus. Numerous word problems. 1978.

Problem Solving

Do you find problems, or do you identify solutions? To make a significant contribution to your organization, develop effective problem-solving techniques and learn to solve problems before they become crises.

> Managers don't have problems. Managers solve problems.
>
> Bernard Schulman,
> President,
> Hot Pink Party Services, Inc.

Techniques draw from other skill areas, such as creativity, math formulas, and group processes, but they all begin in the same place, isolating the problem from the symptoms.

Once the problem has been identified, write a problem statement, for example: "how can we increase our publicity?" Use a wide range of methods to discover solutions. The following ideas will help you initiate the process.

Activities

Remember Murphy's Law, "Anything that can go wrong will go wrong"? It's easier to avoid problems than to solve them, and you can do this by anticipating everything that could potentially go wrong and developing alternatives.

In *A Whack on the Side of the Head,* Roger von Oech suggests that you use creativity to discover new solutions by looking for more than one answer, changing your questions, and challenging the rules.

Seeking just one answer to your problem may cause you to miss out on potential solutions. Generate as many alternatives as possible by rephrasing the initial question in the plural: "What are the answers to the problem?"

Your search for solutions may be too narrow, based on your problem statement. Broadening you question will allow you to generate different resolutions. For example, if employees are unhappy with their present compensation, the question, "How much of an increase will the employees accept?" narrows the solution to salary; maybe the employees would be satisfied with different or better benefits. So a more productive question would be, "What benefit options would appeal to the employees?"

Don't miss out on new approaches by being a stickler in following the rules. If you can get rid of preconceived notions on how business must be done and has always been done, you'll open yourself up to new ways to speed up the process, cut through the bureaucracy, increase efficiency, and solve your problems more effectively.

Use the resources listed below as well as those in the creativity and math sections to develop your problem-solving skills.

Audiocassette Programs

Creative Problem Solving
American Management Association
Extension Institute
Box 1026
Saranac Lake, NY 12983-9986
(518) 891-5510

An audiocassette workbook program, including six cassettes and workbook with quizzes and exercises, structured to help you solve problems by renewing your powers of creativity. Course service staff available to grade quizzes and provide feedback. One Continuing Education Unit (CEU) available upon completion.

Books

*Practical Management Problem
  Solving and Decision Making*
Richard Lyles
Robert E. Krieger Publishing Co.,
  Inc.
Box 9542
Melbourne, FL 32902-9542
(407) 724-9542
Presents a different approach to deci-
sion making, the Lyles Method, with
six steps for decision making and sev-
en stops for problem solving. Worth-
while guide that defines and works
through the processes. 1982.

*Techniques of Structured
  Problem Solving*
Arthur B. Van Gundy, Jr.
Van Nostrand Reinhold Co., Inc.
Division of Thomson Publishing
  Corp.

115 Fifth Ave.
New York, NY 10003
(800) 926-2665
Features 70 individual and group techniques providing a base to select and
utilize techniques for potential solutions. 1988.

A Whack on the Side of the Head
Roger von Oech
Warner Books, Inc.
666 Fifth Ave.
New York, NY 10103
(212) 484-2900; (800) 638-6460
Highly recommended, clever, insightful
book filled with stories, exercises, visuals, and ideas for approaching problem solving creatively. 1990.

Speaking

What's the number one phobia in America? It has been said that
individuals dread speaking before a group more than they fear death
and financial ruin. If the thought of speaking to a group causes your
limbs to tremble and your jaw to clamp shut, you've missed opportunities to deliver your message. Great ideas are just ideas unless you
communicate them to others and convert them into action.

> The mind is a wonderful thing. It starts working the
> minute you're born and never stops until you get up to
> speak in public.
>
> Jacob M. Braude

If you want to succeed, you must developed effective verbal
communication skills. The ability to speak well, whether to individuals
or a group, enhances all of your other skills and empowers you to
inform, persuade, and influence others. Don't let sweaty palms and
heart palpitations dissuade you from learning this skill.

There are basic differences and similarities in the different types of speech. Communicating one-on-one is interactive while communicating to a group is one way. Basic principles, such as knowing your material and audience and being prepared, apply to all types of speaking.

Think before you speak. Prior to attending a meeting, review the meeting purpose and what information will come up and plan for a potential contribution. Know the individuals you will speaking with and think how you will tell them what you want them to hear, but in their language and their terms. A formal speech requires extensive planning and preparing, in both structure and content. How will you grab the audience's attention, develop rapport, make the information relevant, set the proper tone, and develop a relationship?

> It's not just what you know, but how you communicate it. Communication is the most critical management tool. If people don't have these skills, they are at a disadvantage in getting where they'd like to go in their careers and in helping their organization reach its goals. Communication skills have immense pay-offs, not only on the job, but everywhere in your life. The better your communication skills, the better the rewards.
>
> James Anderson,
> *Speaking to Groups: Eyeball to Eyeball*

You can be a better speaker and communicator by understanding basic speech principles and applying them through practice.

Practice by rehearsing your speech in front of the mirror, with a tape recorder, in front of others, and using a video camera. Check your posture, facial expressions and overall body language in front of the mirror. A tape recorder, by itself or in front of the mirror, provides a check on your voice and speech content. It has the advantage of allowing playbacks and monitoring and hearing improvements. Speaking in front of others and receiving their feedback works best if the audience is objective. Family and close friends are often either too critical or not critical enough. Choose professional colleagues or co-workers who can offer honest, helpful suggestions. A videotape gives both audio and visual feedback of your speech or speaking style and is the most effective way to practice. You'll be able to critique your delivery and voice and make improvements.

(continues)

Activities

Reading books gives you the basic principles of speech and lays the foundation for acquiring the skill, but reading alone won't make you a better speaker. You'll need to apply the information by practicing. The more you speak, the better you'll be.

Take a course in improving your speech. It will provide structure and the chance to practice. Look for courses titled "Oral Communications," "Effective Speaking Skills," "Effective Presentation Skills," and "Platform Skills" offered through adult and continuing education programs, private training organizations, and speaking clubs. Ask for recommendations from colleagues and friends, and choose one that is interactive, includes videotaping, and has instructors who are willing to tailor the class to the students' needs.

Take advantage of every opportunity to speak, at business, community, religious, and social group meetings. Express your ideas and opinions.

Joining a speakers program is a sociable and helpful way to improve and practice your speech. Toastmasters International is a nonprofit organization with 7,000 Toastmasters clubs located in 50 countries. It offers an ongoing series of experiences to improve communication skills. If there's no local speakers program, start a support group yourself after completing a course. Enlist other attendees to continue meeting, lending support, and critiquing speeches.

Investigate and participate in an in-house speakers bureau. Many large organizations set up speaker's bureaus to help employees develop skills to communicate with the general public while providing speakers to community and civic organizations.

If you find you need a more individualized approach, a private coach provides one-on-one attention and focuses specifically on your personal needs. This method can be quite effective, but it is also the most expensive method of improvement.

The following resources will start you on the road to better verbal communications.

Audiocassette Programs

Getting Up to Speak!
American Management
  Association
Extension Institute
Box 1026
Saranac Lake, NY 12983-9986
(518) 891-5510

An audiocassette workbook program, including six cassettes and workbook with quizzes and exercises, designed to help you master public speaking skills. Includes organizing your ideas, conquering fear, attention grabbers, effective body language and gestures. Course service staff available to grade quizzes and provide feedback. 1 Continuing Education Unit (CEU) available upon completion.

How to Speak Persuasively
American Management
  Association
[see above]

An audiocassette workbook program, including six cassettes and workbook with quizzes and exercises, designed to help you influence others by developing persuasive powers through targeted speaking techniques. Course service staff available to grade quizzes and provide feedback. One Continuing Education Unit (CEU) available upon completion.

Never be Nervous Again
Dorothy Sarnoff With
  Gaylen Moore
CareerTrack
3085 Center Green Dr.
Boulder, CO 80301-5408
(303) 440-7440; (800) 334-1018

Six audiocassettes and guide designed to help you speak with confidence one-on-one or to groups. Effective techniques and tips to convey your message.

Books

The Little Black Book of Business Speaking
Michael C. Thomsett
AMACOM Books
135 W. 50th St.
New York, NY 10020
(212) 586-8100

Comprehensive book dealing with overcoming nervousness and improving platform skills. Includes preparation, understanding the audience, nonverbal communication, props, and handling different speaking situations. Work projects follow each chapter. 1989.

Never Be Nervous Again
Dorothy Sarnoff
Crown Publishers, Inc.
225 Park Ave. S.
New York, NY 10003
(212) 254-1600

Excellent book showing how effective speech can positively affect all areas of your life. First hand experiences, user friendly format, and checklists make it easy to read. Includes preparation, rehearsing, delivery, appearance, and how to make the most of all speaking situations by turning nervousness into enthusiasm. 1987.

Speaking to Groups Eyeball to Eyeball
James B. Anderson
Wyndmoor Press, Inc.
Box 2105
Vienna, VA 22183
(800) 869-0788

From beginner to expert, this excellent guide gives you the confidence to succeed. Exercises and information will improve your self-confidence and help you achieve winning techniques for speaking success. 1989.

Self-Study Programs

How to Deliver Winning Presentations
American Management
  Association
Extension Institute
Box 1026
Saranac Lake, NY 12983-9986
(518) 891-5510

Six chapters of self-paced study enable you to speak effectively by learning how to organize your ideas, integrate visuals and body language, and build rapport with audiences. Course service staff support, objective test, and case study. Earn two Continuing Education Units (CEUs).

Videos

Confident Public Speaking
Roko Paskov
CareerTrack
3085 Center Green Dr.
Boulder, CO 80301-5408
(303) 440-7440; (800) 334-1018
Two-part program offering techniques enhancing speaking skills by relation exercises, voice exercises, facial expressions, tips and ideas to spice up presentations, and more.

Speakers' Organizations

Toastmasters International
Box 10400
2200 N. Grand Ave.
Santa Ana, CA 92711
(714) 542-6793
Membership organization for adults interested in improving oral communications and developing leadership skills. Offers Communication and Leadership Program manual and an Advanced Communication and Leadership program.

Writing

Do you want to convey original ideas, a fresh perspective, or an innovative approach? Whatever your goal—to persuade, convince, sell, or motivate—clear and concise writing gets your message across.

Effective writing is natural, easy to read, and easy to understand. Build your strengths in clarity, conciseness, organization, spelling, grammar, and punctuation. You'll express yourself well and gain visibility, too.

Writing is developed in three stages: researching, drafting, and editing.

Research involves reading, gathering data, sorting ideas, and brainstorming. Use whatever organizational methods work for you, whether it's taking notes in a notebook or on individual note cards, making copies, or highlighting text. Keep all reference materials together in a folder or file.

What is the purpose of your writing? Do you want to persuade, convince, or inform? Identify and understand your audience. Writing that lacks purpose and direction won't achieve your goals.

It's helpful to begin with a brief outline of your thoughts and ideas. You'll need some type of structure or blueprint to highlight your main points. Write your first draft quickly, capturing your excitement on paper. Don't worry about the sentence structure and spelling; these steps are part of the editing process. You'll organize and reorganize your ideas in the drafting stage, so expect to write multiple drafts. The more you write and rewrite, the more effective your final product.

Give yourself a break between the drafting and editing stages and you'll view your writing with a fresh and renewed perspective. Fine tune your product during the editing stage, identifying and correcting organizational problems. You'll trim and substitute words, correct spelling and grammatical errors, reorganize, and make it better, the same way you improve your landscaping by trimming and pruning the shrubs and replacing tired plantings. Meticulous care takes time and attention and is evident in the end product.

Activities

You can become a better writer by performing the following activities.

Become an insatiable reader. Read all different kinds of materials: newspapers, newsletters, biographies, science fiction, novels, magazines, whatever appeals to you. You'll become familiar with different styles of writing and learn useful information.

Learn and apply the cornerstone of communication: grammar. Take a course in grammar, read and study a book on the subject, and memorize the principles.

Improve and increase your vocabulary by using a variety of dictionaries and resources. Never read without a dictionary. Look up any word you don't know and add new words to your vocabulary every day. Expand the variety and depth of your vocabulary with a synonym dictionary and a thesaurus.

Write as often as you can and your writing will not only continue to get better, it will get easier. A musician practices scales and a ballerina practices pliés; a writer practices writing by writing. Remember the old saying, Practice Makes Perfect.

Just as the gardener needs proper tools to work, you need a basic dictionary, synonym dictionary or thesaurus, and grammatical and writing guides. Add a technical dictionary and other references that are appropriate for your field.

The following reference books and guides are the basic tools you'll need to cultivate your writing skills.

Audiocassette Programs

Business Writing Skills
Debra Smith
CareerTrack
3085 Center Green Dr.
Boulder, CO 80301-5408

(303) 442-0392; (800) 334-1018
Four audiocassettes covering letters, proposals, and memos and how to develop techniques and tips to write more easily and effectively.

Books (Reference)

A Writer's Reference
Diana Hacker
Bedford Books
St. Martin's Press, Inc.
175 Fifth Ave.
New York, NY 10010
(212) 674-5151; (800) 221-7945
Excellent spiral-bound reference, conveniently used at the computer or typewriter. Well organized, easy to use with multiple indexes and cross-references. Includes composing and writing, working on a word processor, grammatical sentences, effective sentences, word choice, punctuation, mechanics, documentation, and basic grammar review. 1989.

The Elements of Style
William Strunk and E. B. White
MacMillan Publishing Co.
Front & Brown Sts.
Riverside, NJ 08075
(800) 257-5755
Excellent resource for the elementary rules of usage, principles of composition, commonly misused words and expressions, and stylistic approaches. 1979.

Katharine Gibbs Handbook of
    Business English
Michelle Quinn
[see above]
Excellent reference, both comprehensive and easy to use, includes information on usage, grammar, and structure. Extensive cross-references and index. 1987.

The Synonym Finder
J. I. Rodale
Warner Books
666 Fifth Ave.
New York, NY 10103
(212) 484-2900; (800) 638-6460
The very best resource for synonyms. Organized alphabetically includes more than 1 million synonyms with separate divisions for different parts of speech and different meanings of the same word. 1978.

Books (Writing Guides)

Business Writing Quick & Easy
Laura Brill
AMACOM Books
135 W. 50th St.
New York, NY 10020
(212) 586-8100
Easy-to-follow and practical guide to writing more effectively. Filled with examples and exercises covering all aspects of business writing. 1989.

The Little Black Book of
    Business Letters
Michael C. Thomsett
AMACOM Books
[see above]
Quick guide filled with directions, examples, and exercises for major types of business letters. 1988.

Plain Letters
Federal Stock No. 7610-00-205-1091
U.S. Government Printing Office
Washington, DC 20402
(202) 783-3238
Insightful, interesting, easy to read book based on the principle that good letters are plain letters. Dozens of makeovers demonstrate how to improve/strengthen your writing. Includes Watchlist, overworked words and phrases with alternative choices. 1955. Recently updated.

Write to the Point!
Rosemary T. Fruehling and
  N. B. Oldham
McGraw-Hill Book Co.
1221 Avenue of the Americas
New York, NY 10020
(212) 512-2000
Excellent guide to developing effective business writing skills. Covers basic grammar, punctuation, and letter elements for writing business letters, memos, and reports. 1988.

Writing With Precision
Jefferson Bates
Acropolis Books
11741 Bowman Green Dr.
Reston, VA 22090
(703) 709-0006; (800) 451-7771
Excellent guide to improving your written communications including information on grammar, revising and editing, and letter, memo, and report writing. Filled with exercises that help you apply the principles and strengthen your writing. 1985.

Computer Software

RightWriter
Que Software
11711 N. College Ave.
Carmel, IN 46032
(317) 573-2500

Grammar and style checking software for the IBM PC, PC AT, PS/2 and compatible personal computers, Macintosh, DeskMate UNIX and Network. Proofreads documents for punctuation errors, wrong words, redundancy, and grammatical problems. Detects more than 25,000 writing errors using advanced parsing and artificial intelligence. Summarizes document for overall writing readability, strength of delivery, and descriptiveness. Copy of *The Elements of Style* included. Features "hot key" access to six best-selling word processing software programs. System requirements: PC DOS or MS-DOS 2.0 or higher. 1990.

Self-Study Programs

Write to the Point!
American Management
  Association
Extension Institute
Box 1026
Saranac Lake, NY 12983-9986
(518) 891-5510
Approximately twenty hours of self-paced study providing guidelines, techniques, and exercises to improve your memos, reports, and proposals. Course service staff support, objective test, and case study. Earn two Continuing Education Units (CEU).

Ten Ways to Acquire Skills

Skills can be obtained any time, anywhere, and in almost any situation. You can learn in traditional workshops, at home, at work, on a computer, or in another work or office setting. Learn on your own and set your pace of work with others. Choose from the following opportunities that meet your lifestyle and preferences.

(continues)

1. *Volunteering*. Nonprofit organizations that serve the public to better the quality of life are always looking for volunteers. While offering your time and services without compensation will help others, you too can reap the benefits. Contribute your time to an organization and pick up new skills or strengthen existing ones. Volunteering is a way to test the waters and try something new. You can afford to be creative and take more risks.

   The over 300 to 400 volunteer centers in the United States, with a primary goal of promoting volunteerism in the community, will match potential volunteers with organizations. To find volunteer centers in your community, contact:

   The National Volunteer Center
   111 N. 19th St., Ste. 500
   Arlington, VA 22209
   (703) 276-0542.

2. *On-the-Job Training*. Employers offer diverse opportunities to learn while performing work responsibilities. You'll find formal instructional programs, such as self-paced, classroom, and computerized programs, as well as informal, such as procedural and training manuals and peer and supervisory assistance.

3. *Shadowing*. Shadowing is a short-term opportunity for you to see and learn firsthand what a job is all about. You'll spend a specific amount of time with a professional in a position of interest to you, see what the work responsibilities are and how they're handled. You may even get a chance to handle some tasks yourself.

   Your present organization may offer shadowing. Some colleges, alumnae groups, and community organizations offer these opportunities and call them "externships." Use them to explore a career field, industry, or organization.

4. *Workshops*. Workshops are structured groups that exchange ideas and practical methods. Productive workshops have a set agenda and realistic goals.

   You'll find workshop offerings through associations, private training companies, consultants, as well as public school systems and colleges and universities.

5. *College courses*. College courses can be taken traditionally on campus and nontraditionally through correspondence study, night school, summer school, weekend school, exams, credit for life experience, and equivalency exams. New innovations

include online degree programs available for bachelor and masters degrees. Locate colleges and programs through:

Bear's Guide to Earning
  College Degrees
  Non-Traditionally
[*Available only by mail*]
F. & K. Costedoat
Box 826-T
Benicia, CA 94510

Guides you through the maze of nontraditional education from schools and programs, alternative methods of earning credit, and specialized nontraditional schools and programs. Information on degrees, evaluating schools, accreditation, applying, scholarships, and financial aid. Extensive bibliography and resources. 1988.

College Degrees by Mail
John Bear
Ten Speed Press
Box 7123
Berkeley, CA 94707
(415) 845-8414

Excellent guide to over 100 schools that offer degrees by mail. Filled with advice and valuable information including ways of earning credit, checking out schools, and how to apply. Numerous appendices. 1991.

6. *Adult Education.* Adult education courses are offered during the day, evenings, and week-ends, and are sponsored by the public school system, business schools, and privately owned schools. Courses can be short, two to six hours, or cover anywhere from five to twenty weeks, and are usually noncredit.

7. *Apprenticeship.* Apprenticeship programs, available mainly for industrial and craft occupations, combine formal classroom study with supervised on-the-job training. Apprentices receive a salary while participating in the programs. Training periods average one to six years.

8. *In-House Training.* Training departments coordinate workshops, lectures, and seminars, at no cost to the employee, to develop and improve skills.

   Find out what programs your organization offers, any prerequisites, and the registration process by checking with your manager of the corporate training department. In-house training is an excellent and convenient way to build your skills.

9. *Home-Study Courses.* Home study provides the opportunity for the student to study on their own by enrolling and studying with an educational institution providing lesson materials prepared in a sequential and logical order. The student completes the lessons and either mails or makes available the assigned work for correction, grading, comment, and subject-matter

guidance by qualified instructors. Corrected assignments are returned to the student. The courses vary greatly in scope, level, and length.

Home-study courses prepare you for upgrading in your present job and provide vocational training. The school comes to you, allowing you to increase your knowledge and skill to your own pace.

National Home Study Council
1601 Eighteenth St. NW
Washington, DC 20009
(202) 234-5100
Offers: *Directory of Accredited Home Study Schools, Studying at Home for College Credit, What Does Accreditation Mean to You? You and Home Study,* and *Facts About the National Home Study Council.*

MacMillan Guide to Correspondence Study
MacMillan Publishing Co.
866 Third Ave.
New York, NY 10022
(212) 702-2000

Lists accredited programs offered through colleges/universities, proprietary programs, private, nonprofit, government institutions, and computer-based programs. Describes courses offered, admissions procedures, and includes subject index.

10. *Cooperative Education.* Cooperative education combines academic study and career interests with actual paid work experiences. This program integrates the educational and employment experiences, building work experiences for future job success and financially assisting the student during the educational process.

For further information, contact the cooperative education department or the admission department at the college of interest or contact:

National Commission for Cooperative Education
360 Huntington Ave.
Boston, MA 02115
(617) 437-3778

Chapter 6

Making Contacts

Where do you go when you need the latest data for your report? How do you determine which software program will meet your business needs? How do you find out about job opportunities?

Interacting with others provides information that helps you do your job, anticipate and plan career growth, and assists you in achieving your career goals. Making contact with others expands your options and enables you to access resources and people when you need them. A network of contacts is your best and most effective tool for achieving your career goals.

People don't go to business meetings, parties, and conventions to meet delightful charming people. They go to work. To pick up useful gossip and display their devotion to their jobs, to make new contacts and renew old ones, to publicize their latest triumph and to squelch the latest slander. . . . You have to be a player to get into the game.

Katha Pollitt,
American writer

Contacts will not come to you; you must take the initiative. You have to actively pursue, make, and build your connections. Connecting works best when you choose activities, individuals, and groups and commit to participation and cultivation of these resources.

The opportunities and ways to connect are limited only by your imagination. It's possible to access people and information through professional and trade associations, unions, groups, networks, computer bulletin boards, conferences, meetings, workshops, speeches, classes, and lectures. View every personal exchange as a link to information and re-sources.

The best jobs are those are found through networking. Mike Townshend, Vice-President of New Options Group, Inc., an outplacement firm, found through surveys that 67 to 70 percent of his company's clients found their jobs through networking, while only 10 to 12 percent of their clients found their jobs through the newspaper employment classified section. As Mike explains it:

> Companies are concerned that the people they hire be not only qualified in a technical way, but also have a good reputation for being successful at what they do. It is very difficult to get a good job reference because companies, avoiding the risk of litigation, seem to give bland recommendations. If a person is referred to a job opportunity by someone who knows them and can attest to their contributions, there is a validation on the table of that individual's worth. Companies have a desire to hire people that they can find out something about, and the most logical way to do this is for them to accomplish this is by networking.

> Another consideration is financial. Every other recruitment method costs money and networking is the least expensive way for companies to hire people. There is a growing pattern in companies to recruit by networking and you'll find them increasing their employee referral programs, financial incentive programs for current employees to refer job candidates.

> Networking is the number one way to find a job.

John Rupple, National Account Manager, WYNDGATE Technologies, Inc., discusses the value of networking:

> I made a grave mistake in my last job and I have learned from it. When I first started working there I went to lunch every day with different people and established a wonderful network. I kept track of these people as they worked for other organizations and different industries. But, as a result of all of those lunches, I began to put on weight. My back began to hurt and the doctor I consulted suggested I begin a daily exercise routine.

> We had a gym at our office and I began exercising during the lunch hour and eventually I eliminated going out to lunch. I severed my network. People got upset because I wouldn't go out to lunch and even though I suggested

breakfast or a drink, I would only go out once or twice a month. My network collapsed. I lost all the weight and my connections at the same time.

Part of my job was meeting with the presidents and chief financial officers of large banks all over the United States. It never occurred to me to pursue and foster those relationships. The seeds were there but I omitted watering them. I have since learned that you have to work at business relationships and I realize now how important that is. As a result of a corporate reorganization, I sent out numerous résumés and only got a few nibbles.

Networking is so very valuable and key in this job market and economy. If you don't do it, it's suicidal. Now, I make an effort. I work out in the morning, and only occasionally during lunch time. I go out to lunch two or three times a week and network regularly. I read *The Wall Street Journal* every day. It gives me fuel for conversation, something to use to find someone's hot button. I have learned from my mistakes and will not put myself in the same position again.

Who Is in Your Present Network?

Even if you have never actively networked, you already have an established network of contacts. It is just a matter of identifying (see box) and tapping into it.

Networks

1. Your family: your parents, spouse, siblings, aunts, uncles, cousins, other relatives, and their networks.
2. Your friends, neighbors, former neighbors, and their networks.
3. Your former classmates and their parents, teachers, guidance and career counselors, alumni, fraternity and sorority members, and their networks.
4. Your present and former employers, colleagues, supervisors, subordinates, customers, clients, suppliers, competitors, and their networks.
5. Your present and former professional and trade association and union members, board of directors, staff, and their networks.
6. Your lawyer, accountant, doctors, dentists, clergy, insurance agents, bankers, and their networks.

7. Your plumber, painter, electrician, hairdresser, dry cleaner, other service workers, and their networks.
8. Your local librarian, public officials, and their networks.
9. The store owners and salespeople in the stores you frequent and their networks.
10. Any clubs, club members, and enthusiasts who share your personal interests and hobbies and their networks.

Lisa H., recent job seeker, described how networking worked for her:

> I started to talk to people I knew and they gave me names of other people and so on. I heard about opportunities and good paying positions. I kept networking and calling people and it was amazing how willing people were to talk to me. I called one woman and she said "You really shouldn't talk to me, you should talk to my husband." I called him and he not only agreed to see me, he gave me fifteen additional names.
>
> I proceeded to do a little script. I called people and nine out of ten returned my call, talked with me, and I went to see them. I got the opportunity to find out about organizations and obtained numerous interviews.
>
> A friend told me about a wonderful job. I've met with the firm and found we have a lot in common. I'm presently negotiating a contract. I have an interview tomorrow with another organization, just in case this doesn't work out. If none of it comes through, I have another list of names for a second wave of phone calls.

How to Connect

You must develop a plan to connect and meet people. This isn't as difficult as it sounds because the opportunities to network are all around you. Choose the ones that fit your schedule, personality, and lifestyle. The activities listed here work best if you remember to be an initiator. Don't wait to be introduced or for others to speak to you. Introduce yourself and initiate a conversation.

1. Join at least one professional or trade association in your field or field of interest. Attend meetings and target making one new contact per meeting. Volunteer to work on committees or participate in special interest groups. The more active you are, the more contacts you will make. Before joining a group,

request an information packet and know what services the organization provides for membership dues. Assess which organization provides information and resources that best meet your needs.

2. Attend half-day-, day-, or week-long conferences. Introduce yourself to speakers and attendees. Obtain lists of attendees and speakers and plan on keeping in touch.

3. Consider professional development programs an opportunity not only to increase your skills and knowledge, but to expand your network.

4. Join traditional professional groups such as fraternal, community, and business groups and clubs.

5. Attend short programs and speeches in areas of interest sponsored by networking groups, adult and continuing education, alumnae associations, professional and trade associations, and community and governmental organizations. Make contact with attendees, speakers and sponsors.

6. Get involved with your alumni association. Pursue local chapters or set one up yourself. Submit current information concerning your career achievements to the alumni association and followup with other alumni in your interest area.

7. Keep in touch with professors and instructors of college, university, and adult and continuing education courses.

8. Offer to participate in user groups and committees in your organization. Be open to working with members of different departments and divisions within your organization.

9. Write to authors of books and articles in your field. Establish and pursue a connection.

10. Contribute articles to journals and newsletters of trade and professional associations. Connect with the editors, staff, and readers.

Steps to Developing a Network

There's no clear-cut formula for networking success. You'll do better if you develop a tracking system and procedure for updating, expanding, and keeping up with your growing network of contacts.

1. Create a system for keeping track of your network of connections. Use a Rolodex or card file system that's easily updated and update it regularly. Keep track of contact name, organization, position title, address, work and home phone numbers.

2. Always carry and use business cards. If your organization

doesn't have business cards, order your own. Make it a habit to collect business cards and establish a system for filing them. You can purchase a variety of cases that have plastic sleeves to slip the cards in.

3. Clip articles of interest to your contacts and periodically send them along with a short note.

4. Plan on meeting your contacts regularly for breakfast, lunch, or after-work drinks, whatever fits into your schedule.

5. Invite your contacts to attend professional meetings, programs, and speeches.

6. Recommend and exchange resources. Pass along book and computer software reviews, newsletters, newspapers, reports, and program materials.

7. Introduce your different contacts to each other and let others know you are open and interested in meeting new people.

8. When looking for information, request recommendations and introductions from your contacts.

9. Follow up appropriately and express appreciation. Send thank-you notes and small gifts or take your contacts out to lunch.

10. Keep your eyes and ears open to your contacts' news. Send notes of congratulations for promotions, new jobs, new accounts or contracts, publications, and any noteworthy event. Send notes of encouragement and sympathy when appropriate.

Bruce Crockett, President and Chief Operating Officer, Comsat Corporation, explains that networking is a conscious effort:

Networking is not something that happens naturally; you have to have a plan to do it. No one is going to do it for you, no one is going to look out for you like you—the onus is on you.

You need to know peers within your industry, within your specialty, in other industries, and in geographical regions so you can help yourself as well as help others. Networking is a two-way street.

There really is no magic to it but some people are better at it than others. Networking has to be purposeful and it has to be planned. You almost have to add it to your list as one of the ten things you plan to do today.

I keep a list of key people I know in various industries and adjust the list periodically based on who is doing what, who has retired, and who has moved up. These are people I think are important to me or who could be important in certain situations. I have a master list of people I want to know and people I want to have access to if I need them at a specific time. Most of these people are ones I have had experience with over the years and a cumulative list of people I have known in the business environment who were excellent and important.

I keep in touch with my contacts in different ways. Sometimes I send them a note, sometimes a holiday card, sometimes I don't talk to them at all. I don't sit down and decide I'll spend one hour networking today. But I keep my list so I don't forget about them. I periodically review my list and decide who, when, and how I should contact.

Networking and the Job Search

The best way to find a job is through your network and the best time to establish a network is when you are not looking for a job. It's hard to cultivate individuals and build on relationships when you're very needy. So what do you do if you don't have an existing network and you need a job?

Relax. You have an existing network, whether or not you've been actively cultivating and building one. If you haven't been using yours, it's time to activate it.

Nancy Schuman, Vice-President, Marketing and Operations, at Career Blazers Personnel Services, a permanent and temporary placement firm, suggests:

Tell every person that you know that you are looking for a job. Tell friends, tell family, tell someone that works at a company you would like to work for, or has a thread of a connection. Try to get the person that you know who knows someone who works there to get you an introduction.

I think contacts are great because they can give you names of people who are working at a company or they can tell you typically how a company pays, what the internal structure is like, or the hiring structure, or when there are internal openings or promotions that no one else would know about.

Networking is a great way to find jobs. I think people are embarrassed to tell people that they are job hunting or afraid to take advantage of people who know other people. If someone says to me. "I have a friend or cousin that would be great in your business and is really interested, would you be interested in meeting them?" I would absolutely meet that person based on my friend's evaluation of them. People should take advantage of that.

Before we begin to identify your network, let's look at how this process works in the job search. Networking for job leads is a multiplication game. As you use the telephone to call your contacts and personal referrals, you'll build on these calls and contacts to identify more contacts and make more phone calls, leading to information about job openings. The more phone calls and contacts you make, the greater your odds at finding a job by networking.

All of this calling and contacting can be confusing and you'll be more successful if you follow an organized, systematic approach. Begin the process by brainstorming, identifying, and listing your existing network using the ideas listed earlier in the chapter under "Who Is in Your Present Network." You'll be calling individuals on your list and asking them if they know of any job opportunities. Keep adding to your list of contacts by setting yourself a goal of obtaining two additional names from every contact you make. The statistics are in your favor; the more calls and leads, the greater your chance of finding opportunities that haven't been published.

Calling strangers to ask for help can unnerve even the most confident. While you'll probably encounter some resistance, you'll be surprised how helpful people can be, after all, it's human nature for people to help other people. You've helped others before and think how much more helpful and sympathetic you'll be in the future when others call upon your support.

Handle your calls in a businesslike fashion and avoid putting the contact on the defensive by asking for a job. Do this by stating who you are, who referred you, and what you do. Ask about openings and opportunities in your defined profession and geographic area. Follow these questions by querying about openings in the contact's organization. Develop a script that goes like this:

> "Hello Ms. Armstrong, my name is David Irwin. Jane Roberts recommended I call you. I'm an internal auditor.
> "I am presently looking for an internal auditing position in private industry. Do you know of any openings or opportunities in the Dallas/Fort Worth area or in your own organization?"

If the answer is yes, get the names of contacts, their organizations, and phone numbers. If the answer is no, you can still follow up with, "Do you know of someone else who may be able to help me?" Build on your successes and don't dwell on any failures. The more people you reach, the closer you'll get to the job that's right for you.

An efficient way to maintain your growing database of information is to use a cross-referenced card system. Create two cards for every call, one by the contact name and one by the organization name: this way you'll avoid the embarrassment of forgetting what company the contact works for. Include the contact name, organization, phone number, and referral on each card. Add any additional information such as job leads or further contacts and file the cards alphabetically for easy access. Remember to keep your call short, handle yourself professionally, and be gracious and appreciative. Follow up special support and assistance with a written thank-you note. If someone has been particularly helpful, keep him or her updated regarding your progress.

You'll need to be diligent, persistent, and patient. Always remember, employers are receptive to this type of search. Eventually, you'll make the right call, find the right lead, and successfully complete your job search.

Once you have achieved success, resolve to continue to build, add, and nurture your network. Give help as freely as others have assisted you. You'll reap the benefits throughout your career.

Getting the Most From Networking

Specific, effective techniques enable you to get mileage from your network activities.

How to Strengthen Your Networking Techniques

1. Network all the time and meet as many people as you can. You never know who will have the information or know the contact you'll need now or in the future.
2. Always tell individuals what you do. Create an introductory scenario to use: "Hi. My name is Rose Arthur. I'm a writer with Associated Press."
3. Keep adding to your network. Your opportunities for contacts, resources, and opportunities increase along with the size of your network.
4. Follow up with your contacts. If you've met someone you'd like to know better or someone who has information or resources you need, make a date for lunch, follow up with a phone call, or send on a note or an interesting article.
5. When attending functions, act like a host rather than a guest. Adele Scheele makes this suggestion in *Skills for Success*. A host takes an active role, introducing themselves and guests and making people comfortable.
6. Be willing to give as well as get. It's part of paying your dues. Pass on help, information, and resources to others in need.

7. While your goal is adding to your network, don't be afraid to streamline yours either. Periodically review your files and remove contacts who are no longer productive.
8. Create a network that is a support system. Willingly help your contacts and don't be afraid to ask your contacts for help.
9. Make an effort to get along with anyone who can help you. Be friendly with your contacts, but don't confuse that with a personal relationship. You don't need to develop your business contacts into best friends.
10. If you think networking is using, you're on the wrong track. Effective, worthwhile networking is a smart way for businesspeople to operate. You'll get information faster, support quicker, and find the pleasure and rewards of sharing professional interests and friendships.

Information about existing groups, associations, and networks is all around. Watch for announcements in the business section of your local paper, community and business calendars; postings on bulletin boards at the library, your organization, community centers, and nonprofit and governmental organizations. Check the classified section of your phone directory under *Associations*. Once you begin to look, you will find information and groups for every area of interest.

Resources

Books

The Complete Job Search Handbook
Howard Figler
Henry Holt & Co., Inc.
115 W. 18th St.
New York, NY 10011
(212) 633-0605
Excellent chapter on detective skills providing ideas on how to develop and cultivate a network. 1988.

Skills for Success
Adele Scheele
Ballantine Books
201 E. 50th St.
New York, NY 10022
(212) 572-2266

Excellent, timeless book on how to use networking for career success and satisfaction. Includes ideas on how to initiate contacts including an innovative party exercise where you play the host, greeting and introducing people and taking an active role. 1979.

Computer Software

The Career Management Partner
Scientific Systems
Five Science Park
New Haven, CT 06511
(203) 786-5236
Fully integrated software job search program for the IBM PC and compatibles enabling the user to build and maintain a network. Access to on-line

databases, for example, *Dow Jones News Retrieval, Dialog,* and *Dow Jones Information Services.* Features database of names and addresses including computerized mailing list of 100+ recruiters, word processing, letter and résumé templates, statistically tracks letters and measures response to job campaigns, electronic mail, and information retrieval.

Directories

The following directories identify established professional groups for a wide range of interests.

Directory of U.S. Labor Organizations
BNA Books
Distribution Center
300 Rantan Ctr. Pkwy.
CN 94
Edison, NJ 08818
(201) 225-1900
Provides information on AFL-CIO Headquarters, Central Bodies, and alphabetical listing of labor organizations. Includes addresses, phone numbers, and contacts. 1988.

Encyclopedia of Associations Series
Gale Research Co.
835 Penobscot Bldg.
Detroit, MI 48226
(313) 961-2242; (800) 347-GALE
Series of directories with extensive listings of associations. Updated annually.
Volume 1—National Organizations of the United States
Nearly 21,500 national and international nonprofit trade and professional associations, social welfare and public organizations, religious, sports, and hobby groups with headquarters in the United States. Includes contact information, description of activities, publications, computerized services, and convention schedules.
Volume 2—Geographic and Executive Indexes
Indexes alphabetically all associations found in Volume 1 by city and state, including complete addresses, phone numbers, and names of executives and all executives found in Volume 1 alphabetically by surname, including titles, names of organizations, complete addresses, and phone numbers.
Volume 3—New Associations and Projects
Includes all newly found and newly formed associations not listed in Volume 1.
International Organizations
Companion to Volume 1. Includes detailed description and information on over 4,000 international nonprofit membership organizations based outside the United States.
Regional, State, and Local Organizations
Seven-volume guide to over 50,000 regional, state, and local nonprofit membership organizations in all 50 states, D.C., and U.S. territories. Doesn't overlap entries in Volume 1.

Minority Organizations: A National Directory
Garrett Park Press
Garrett Park, MD 20896
(301) 946-2553
Lists 7,700 black and other minority groups. 1987.

National Trade and Professional Associations of the United States
Columbia Books, Inc.

1212 New York Ave. NW
Ste. 330
Washington, DC 20005
(202) 898-0662

A comprehensive directory of more than 6,250 national trade association, labor unions, professional, scientific, or technical societies. The book is revised annually. 1990.

Women's Organizations:
A National Directory
Martha Merrill Doss
Garrett Park Press
Garrett Park, MD 20896
(301) 946-2553

Lists hundreds of organizations many providing career, guidance, and employment services. Organized alphabetically by organization name and includes an index by category. 1986.

Chapter 7

Sharpening Your Job-Hunting Skills

Qualifications alone won't get you a job. You have to develop effective job-hunting techniques and prepare a job-search strategy to win the job that's right for you. You need a combination of job-hunting skills: résumé and cover letter writing, making contacts, uncovering job leads, and interviewing. You can have a wonderful résumé and great job leads, but if you interview poorly, you won't get the job. On the flip side, you might have excellent interview skills but a poor résumé, few contacts, and have little opportunity to put those skills to use.

Carefully plan your job search by deciding up front how much time and effort and what priority you will devote to each segment of the search. Budget your time wisely.

People manage the job search the way they manage their careers. The proactive person is out there working the network and doing the research. People can do a good job of preparing and having the necessary skills, but if they don't show the product of having worked hard to get where they are, I'm not as impressed.

Wade Robinson,
Director Planning and Staffing,
Defense Systems, UNISYS Corporation

Many job seekers feel they lack control in the job-search process. You can win back some of this control and boost your confidence if you assume leadership in detailing a careful plan and strategy. As you begin to see results, your confidence will soar and you will accomplish your goals, securing a job that meets your needs and bring satisfaction.

This chapter and Chapters 8 and 9 provide information, insight, innovative ideas, and resources for résumés, cover letters, federal job applications, job leads, and interviews. Adapt and integrate the information that works best for you and make it part of your job-hunting techniques.

Résumés

Your job search should begin by preparing a résumé. A résumé isn't an autobiography or your memoirs and doesn't include every work and education experience that you've had. Your résumé is an opportunity to assess your credentials and choose those skills, experiences, education, and accomplishments that show your qualifications for the position you seek.

I looked at writing my résumé as a chore but, once I sat down at the computer and started working on it, it became clear what I wanted to do and who I was. The person I was writing about was incredible and it gave me a real boost. I found it hard to do a résumé in a crisis. What you really should do is always have a résumé and build on it so when an opportunity comes up, you're ready.

Lisa H.,
Recent job hunter

In other words, your résumé is the marketing tool you will use to sell your experiences and accomplishments to prospective employers. Your résumé introduces you to employers and they will decide from it whether they would like to meet you and explore your qualifications further. Make that first impression count!

If you are one of those individuals who prefers a root canal to writing your résumé, relax, help is on the way. The following steps show you how to write and produce a winning résumé.

Twelve Steps to Creating an Effective Résumé

1. Using lined paper, begin by outlining all your work experience, paid and nonpaid. Volunteer experience is important. We often choose to spend our free time in activities that give us pleasure and satisfac-

tion. Don't ignore them. Noting these activities may strengthen your credentials.

2. Use a sheet of paper for each job, and list all of your work responsibilities. Look at each responsibility and describe the tasks involved, the problems you encountered, how you solved them, and the outcome. Quantify wherever possible. Did you manage a staff of one or ten? Were you responsible for a budget of $100,000 or $3 million?

3. Choose the type of résumé that highlights and targets your skills for the position you seek. There are two types: chronological and functional.

The chronological is the most traditional, listing experiences and education in date order, beginning with the most recent and working backwards. It works best for individuals who have followed a career path with positions of increased responsibility. Some employers, particularly those in traditional industries or fields such as banking, accounting, or law, will only consider chronological resumes. Use your contacts to check out résumé preferences for organizations you are interested in.

The functional résumé organizes your work history by areas of expertise and experience such as managing, writing, training, marketing, or administering. A work history including places of employment, job titles, and dates is optional. The functional résumé downplays gaps in employment and numerous job moves. It works best for individuals changing careers and transferring skills and experiences from one career to another and for individuals who have changed careers but have not yet established a steady career path.

While functional résumés can be very effective, if at all possible, I would recommend the chronological format, as most interviewers are most comfortable with it. Some employers think you're hiding something when you send a functional résumé. The chronological format quickly and easily highlights your career progress and contributions to a prospective employer.

4. Consider using a Career Summary if you have ten-plus years of work experience. The Career Summary, also called a Background Summary, Qualifications Summary, Career History, Career Highlights, or Summary of Experience, is an opportunity to include up front your strengths, achievements, expertise, and career interests. You can use a career objective as well, but a well-written summary can often combine your career target with your credentials.

5. Your résumé should express your unique skills, abilities, and contributions. Highlight these by creating a format for your résumé. Organize it so that you begin with your strengths and then continue to

build your credentials. Start with a career objective or summary. What strengthens your qualifications? Work experience, education, training, skills, or professional certifications? Include and add these categories in order of desirability.

6. Your résumé must be clear and concise. Write it using the active voice. Misspelled words and grammatical errors are unacceptable: use a dictionary and grammar book to check for errors. Avoid jargon and acronyms. The tenses should all agree. Describe your present experience in the present tense, past experience in the past tense. If you want to list experiences you are no longer handling in a current job, double space and include the past experiences. When using a functional format, group present experiences together and follow with past experiences.

7. Edit your résumé many times to make it as effective as possible. Use a synonym dictionary, thesaurus, and standard dictionary to locate synonyms and improve word choice. What's the most overused word in résumé writing? *RESPONSIBLE.* Don't use it. The words *develop, manage,* and *provide* are also overused. Substitute the following synonyms for these verbs.

Develop

generate	establish	compose	expand	create
enlarge	increase	institute	organize	build
advance	set up	add		

Manage

direct	supervise	lead	plan and	head
administer	oversee	control	direct	guide

Provide

furnish	present	extend	maintain	implement
supply	produce	arrange	oversee	administer

8. Be creative in your résumé layout but remember: your goal is a professional appearance. Balance with bold, uppercase and lowercase, and ruling lines. Choose different sizes and styles of fonts but avoid size extremes. Use bullets to highlight different areas. Make these with a lowercase *o* and fill in carefully with a black felt-tip pen.

9. Keep your résumé to one or two pages in length. If you have

extensive experience and qualifications, it is fine to use two pages. If you have numerous publications, you may need to use three pages, but this is the only exception. When using two pages, never use a two-sided copier and always staple the pages together.

10. Make your résumé easy to read. Allow for at least 1-inch margins on top, bottom, and sides. Avoid long paragraphs and try to balance your white space.

11. Ask a trusted friend to proofread the résumé.

12. Produce your résumé so that it can easily be changed or updated. If you can, use a word processor, word processing software, desktop publishing, or a service that will do it for you. You'll get the best results with a letter quality or laserjet printer. Avoid paper that is flashy and unusual in color, quality, texture, and size. Professional color choices are white, off-white, cream, or beige. Comparison-check prices for copying or printing your résumé.

The following résumé samples provide ideas on how to present and highlight your qualifications. Your personal situation and career direction dictate the type of résumé you use, the format, and the content.

It's helpful not only to look at samples, but to find out the reasons why the individuals chose those specific experiences, résumé type, and format.

What follows are profiles of job seekers and changers. You'll learn about their work histories, career goals, and the decisions they made in writing and formatting their résumés.

Wendy Henderson

Wendy Henderson wanted to work in food management for as long as she could remember. She majored in food service management and after college, began building a career managing restaurants.

She worked hard and moved progressively, assuming responsibility for larger and larger operations. Wendy developed an expertise for opening new establishments and managing them into profitability.

Early in her career, Wendy found out that restaurant management was a seven-day-a-week responsibility. In the beginning, this was a challenge, but lately, it's become a problem. A new husband and an expected addition to the family have caused her to rethink her career goals. Wendy's decided to use her management skills and expertise in another field, one with a work schedule more compatible with her family life.

Figure 4. Sample functional format résumé highlighting skills.

WENDY HENDERSON

10 Pueblo Lane
San Diego, California 92101
(619) 233-0000

Innovative, organized, and successful manager. Nine years experience planning, opening, and managing restaurants from blueprints to profitable operations.

EXPERIENCE

PERSONNEL MANAGEMENT

Hired, trained, and supervised staffs of 20-160. Determined staffing requirements and qualifications, wrote and placed employment advertisements, conducted interviews, and selected employees. Reviewed performance, counseled, and terminated employees. Created training manuals and conducted on-the-job training programs.

- Received awards for outstanding management performance and manager of the year.
- Achieved first place in national contest through employee incentives.

FINANCIAL MANAGEMENT

Created and implemented all financial management systems for organizations generating from $500,000 to $4 million in annual revenue. Developed and installed inventory control, accounts payable, and delivery systems. Researched market, contracted supplies, wrote contracts, and developed cash flow tracking systems. Prepared financial reports for parent company.

- Negotiated best food profit margin in chain.
- Consistently operated one of the top five establishments in chain for profitability.

OPERATIONS MANAGEMENT

Developed sales forecast, staffed restaurant, and ordered supplies to achieve forecasted goals. Created new schedule system that cut waste and substantially lowered labor and food costs.

- Received highest grades in 56 classes of corporate training seminars.
- Consistently achieved best bottom line profit out of 65 restaurants in chain.
- Initiated and implemented a proposal that increased sales by $125,000 per year while dropping costs by $26,000 per year.

WORK HISTORY

Manager, 1988 - present
The Eatery, San Diego, California

Manager, 1984 - 1988
Smith/Hollander, Inc., San Diego, California

Manager, 1983 - 1984
Magic Pan, Denver, Colorado

Manager, 1981 - 1983
Pizza Huts of the Southwest, San Diego, California

Service Director, 1981
Professional Food Service Management, San Francisco, California

EDUCATION

Bachelor of Science, 1980
San Francisco State University, San Francisco, California
Major: Food Service Administration
Minor: Business Administration

Two-year Degree, 1977
Vocational Technical Institute, San Francisco, California
Major: Quantity Food Cookery

Since Wendy planned to transfer her skills, she chose a functional format that would highlight her skills, not job titles or employers (see Figure 4).

She began her résumé with a short and effective introduction that summarized her career highlights. She indicated management experience, which led into the next section, experience.

While personnel, finance, and operations are all part of the management process, Wendy reinforced her management credentials by including the word management in every section heading. It doesn't overwhelm, but, rather, strengthens her credentials.

Wendy included a strong summary in each experience section, quantifying wherever possible. Her accomplishments are separated and highlighted with bullets.

Management experience is further reinforced under the work history. The position titles are in bold while the organizations are deemphasized, in normal type.

Kenneth Long

Kenneth Long worked for eleven years for a Fortune 500 company. He progressed through management, receiving numerous promotions and transfers, developing an expertise in operations management.

In 1977, Kenneth decided it was time to plan a change. His reading and research indicated that the computer industry would continue rapid growth and offered many opportunities. He decided to move into this industry and felt sales was the best way to enter.

Preparing for the change, he requested a move from operations to

(text continues on page 112)

Figure 5. Sample chronological résumé highlighting career profession.

KENNETH LONG
135 Old Georgetown Road, Bethesda, Maryland 20814
(301) 881-0000 (work) (301) 882-0000

BACKGROUND SUMMARY

Senior executive with management background in sales and marketing, finance and operations with organizational responsibility of up to 1,300 people.

Highly successful in creating new business opportunities and turning around existing operations. Most recently led Eastern Software in its highly successful expansion into the Federal Government Market.

Recognized specialist in the government market, identifying and pursuing opportunities and dealing effectively at the senior management level. Developed key business in the commercial and international markets.

EXPERIENCE

VICE PRESIDENT   EASTERN SOFTWARE, INC., 1986 - present

Maintain full general management responsibility for Government Systems Division, with P & L accountability, for a $25 million FY90 business, reporting directly to the President. The Government Systems Division achieved the most successful revenue growth rate and highest profit margins in the company over the past three years.

Accomplishments

Sales and Profits

- Increased sales from an initial flat $3 million level to $25 million level; Government Systems Division sales went from less than 2% of total company business to 15% of total. Obtained $150 million in large government procurements deliverable over next 10 years.

- Generated a 30% return on revenue, the highest in the company, contributing an estimated 25% of total company profits while division's cost of sales are exceptionally low.

Staff Development

- Expanded staff from 11 to over 100, created different compensation program for Government Sales staff, and reduced staff turnover to minimum.

Business Development

- Successfully diversified our position in the Federal market, specifically in consulting services, turnkey systems, qualification as a sole source vendor, and participation in joint proposals for major modernization projects.

- Emphasized efforts to work with individual agencies to standardize on Eastern software.

- Entered into system integration procurement efforts with EDS, General Dynamics, Boeing, and others.

- Developed marketing and advertising programs specifically designed for the government business.

- 11 of the 13 Cabinet-level agencies are Eastern customers, with most IBM data centers using Eastern software.

- Assumed the leadership role in the company for Distribution Management Systems (DMS) installations, selling complete turnkey systems to the GSA warehouses ($15 million in contracts).

REGIONAL MANAGER   NORTHSHARE, INC., 1984 - 1986

Held P&L responsibility for a $10 million, 25-person operation with offices in Washington D.C. and Atlanta. Managed commercial and federal government business for the Mid-Atlantic, Southeast, and Federal Government region for software, consulting, and turnkey systems.

Increased sales from $4 million to $10 million, exceeding plan each year and achieving success in a market (Southeast) in which the company had never been successful.

VICE-PRESIDENT, GENERAL MANAGER   OFFICE SUPPLIERS, INC., 1982 - 1983

Expanded office equipment business to capture federal market. Reorganized the sales operation and increased sales by 35% in just over one year.

DISTRICT MANAGER   COMPUTER SYSTEMS, INC., 1981 - 1982

Assumed responsibility for the Southeast U.S. region for software systems company. Turned around the district, doubled sales volume, established profitability, and opened the Florida market.

ACCOUNT EXECUTIVE   JASS, 1980 - 1981

Marketed application software, financial modeling, and time sharing services in the D.C. and Virginia area for this $40 million company.

NATIONAL ACCOUNT EXECUTIVE   IBM CORPORTION, 1969 - 1980

Promoted to positions of increased responsibility in sales and operations.

As **National Account Executive** for U.S. Department of Justice, increased market share from 30% to 70% through a concentrated effort to establish relationships in the Department and compete aggressively.

OPERATIONS MANAGER

Directed Eastern Distribution Division, an organization with 1,300 people in 9 distribution centers, controlling an operating budget of $35 million. Held operations management positions in administration and refurbished equipment centers.

Assumed full management control in each operation, making significant changes in policies and procedures, organization, personnel, and controls. Moved a center from lowest operational rating to the highest rated operation, reduced personnel turnover from 40-50% to 8-10%, improved asset management, and reduced outstanding receivables.

EDUCATION

Bachelor of Science in Finance, San Diego State University, San Diego, California, 1964

Top Security Clearance

sales. With three years of sales experience to his credit, Kenneth made the move to the computer industry.

Kenneth moved around several times, adding sales and sales management experience to his credentials. He progressed to the Senior Executive level and would like to progress further.

Even though Kenneth had changed careers and industries, he chose a chronological type of résumé, highlighting his career progression (see Figure 5).

He began with a very specific background summary that emphasizes his contributions, accomplishments, and experience.

Kenneth chose to place his job titles in upper case and bold on the left-hand side, with organizations, also in upper case, and employment dates on the right-hand side. This emphasizes the level of experience and reinforces the career progression while downplaying the frequent moves. He used one half of the first page for specific, quantified accomplishments in the area qualifying him for advancement.

Jessica Monroe

Jessica Monroe majored in math in college and decided she wanted to share her love of math through teaching. She began teaching at a middle school and progressed to chair the math department and on to head the school.

After eight years in education, Jessica no longer felt challenged, so she moved to Dallas and began working for Neiman Marcus in a financial position.

Jessica pursued an MBA on a part-time basis while advancing through the financial areas. She realized her goal, passing the CPA exam, the same year she completed the MBA program.

The retail industry has been a prime target of takeovers and leveraged buyouts. Jessica has decided that it's time to make another career move, this time out of her present industry. She's gained lots of valuable experience as well as impressive credentials and feels she's ready to move on.

A chronological résumé works well for Jessica as it highlights her career progression in both organizations (see Figure 6). She knows the areas she's interested in and has written a very specific career objective.

Jessica emphasizes her education credentials and her recently completed MBA by following the Career Objective section with Education.

The organization names have been centered and the job titles placed in upper case and bold on the left-hand side. This further emphasizes the work Jessica has done, as well as her progression. Jessica doesn't feel the descriptions for her positions at Newton School are relevant for further opportunities, so she has only included her job

Figure 6. Sample chronological résumé highlighting progress in two organizations.

JESSICA MONROE, CPA
1590 Cactus Road, Dallas, Texas 75244
(214) 900-2000

CAREER OBJECTIVE

Auditor/Accountant in an organization needing expertise in Audit Management, Data Processing, and Accounting.

EDUCATION

MBA, Finance, Southern Methodist University, Dallas, Texas, 1989
M. Ed, Trinity College, Hartford, Connecticut, Magna Cum Laude,1975
BS, Math, University of Connecticut, Storrs, Connecticut, Cum Laude, 1971

EXPERIENCE

Neiman Marcus, Dallas, Texas, 1981 - present

Financial Control Manager, 1989 - present

Manage accounting and reporting functions for merchandise return area for retail operation with 30 stores. Maintain ledgers, research and resolve discrepancies, and prepare reports for corporate management.

Established audit procedure to monitor data entry of merchandise transfers; identified and corrected errors; reduced shortages by 17%. Developed a report to highlight vendor merchandise refusal; reduced average amount 70% within six months.

Audit Manager, 1984 - 1988

Directed audit program, inventory and expense control, and budgeting. Revised and expanded audit program to improve effectiveness and communication; helped reduce shortage 33% in three years.

Computerized audit programs and reports with personal computers. Improved department's effectiveness and efficiency. New audits could be developed in less time and reports modified more easily to meet management's needs.

Assistant Manager, Data Entry, 1982 - 1983

Managed data processing operations, expense control, and budgeting in two data entry locations with a staff of 40. Tightened operating procedures and restructured the work environment; increased productivity 25% and accuracy 15%.

Assistant Manager, Production Control, 1981 - 1982

Conducted cost analysis and production studies in two service buildings with a staff of five. Updated production standards and improved work methods; increased productivity 10% to 15%.

Newton School, Meriden, Connecticut, 1972 - 1980

Head of Middle School, 1977 - 1980
Chairman, Math Department, 1974 - 1977
Math Instructor, 1972 - 1974

CERTIFICATION

Certified Public Accountant

---

titles and the dates. This also saved space, allowing the résumé to easily fit on one page.

The CPA credentials are important for Jessica's next move. She's included the CPA designation after her name as well as under a heading of certification.

Résumé Aids

Excellent books and software are available to guide you through the writing and producing process. The following list of resources is a sampling of the best.

Books

Damn Good Résumé Guide
Yana Parker
Ten Speed Press
Box 7123
Berkeley, CA 94707
(415) 845-8414

Excellent guide for functional résumés. Good ideas for developing a career objective and career summary, and developing skill directed résumés. 1989.

The Résumé Handbook
Arthur D. Rosenberg &
   David V. Hizer
Bob Adams, Inc.
260 Center St.
Holbrook, MA 02343
(617) 767-8100; (800) 872-5627

Easy to follow guide. Twenty-five examples of effective résumés. Short but good cover letter section. 1990.

Sure-Hire Résumés
Robbie Miller Kaplan
AMACOM Books
135 W. 50th St.
New York, NY 10020
(212) 903-8420

This comprehensive guide is directed to management-level positions. It contains the basics and twenty-five résumé makeovers that graphically show you how to make passable résumés powerful. Includes basic cover letter writing and cover letters written for job openings by top personnel managers. 1990.

Computer Software

RésuméMaker
Individual Software, Inc.
125 Shoreway Rd., Ste. 3000
San Carlos, CA 94070-2704
(800) 874-2042 (CA)
(800) 331-3313 (U.S. except CA)

This résumé program for the IBM PC and Macintosh computers works best if you write and format your résumé first. Very easy to use with excellent documentation, a tutorial on how to use the program, pop-up menus, and on-screen explanations. Offers three types of résumé with seventeen formats, on-line glossary of action words, spell check; custom features allow you to change margins, type styles, positioning or order of paragraphs, text size, and section titles. Built-in word processor, customized cover, thank-you, and broadcast letters; target company database, address book, activities log, and appointment calendar. 1990.

The Résumé Kit
Spinnaker Software
1 Kendall Sq.
Cambridge, MA 02139
(617) 494-9384

This résumé program for the IBM PC works best if you write and format your résumé first. Easy to use with excellent documentation, easy-to-understand help feature and drop-down menus. Automatic formatting includes nine résumé formats, spell check (with 100,000 words) for each screen; custom features allow you to change font, layout, margins, and indentations. Offers letter writing with a built-in word processor, mail merge, and appointment calendar. 1988.

WordPerfect
WordPerfect Corp.
1555 N. Technology Way
Orem, UT 84057
(801) 225-5000

While not a résumé program, this word processing software program will produce a professional looking résumé. It offers desktop publishing capabilities, different fonts, bold, underline, lines, columns, indentations, justification, centering, box text, spell check, and thesaurus. Comes with lifetime toll-free support system and Laserjet support. Documentation is for the word processing program. You will need to learn how to use the program before producing a résumé.

SF-171

Your personal résumé isn't really operable when applying for federal, state, county, and local government jobs. The Standard Form (SF)-171 is the application required to apply for a job with the Federal government (see figure 7). It is the most detailed and comprehensive application and once you have completed this one, you can use the information to complete other applications.

Used for both hiring and advancement, the SF-171 has both similarities and differences to a résumé. The SF-171 is much longer and allows you to include information that, due to page constraints, you are unable to include on a résumé. The work experience sections can be written and formatted as you would a resume.

The SF-171 is a marketing tool just like the résumé. A federal examiner assesses your qualifications based on the job announcement, *X-118 Handbook,* and *Position Classification Standards.*

Terms You Need to Know

position classification standards   Series of manuals published by the Office of Personnel Management defining all jobs in the federal service and providing detailed descriptions of the duties performed

(*text continues on page 122*)

Figure 7. The SF-171 form.

Standard Form 171   Application for Federal Employment

Read The Following Instructions Carefully Before You Complete This Application

- DO NOT SUBMIT A RESUME INSTEAD OF THIS APPLICATION.
- TYPE OR PRINT CLEARLY IN DARK INK.
- IF YOU NEED MORE SPACE for an answer, use a sheet of paper the same size as this page. On **each** sheet write your name, Social Security Number, the announcement number or job title, and the item number. Attach all additional forms and sheets to this application at the top of page 3.
- If you do not answer **all** questions fully and correctly, you may delay the review of your application and lose job opportunities.
- Unless you are asked for additional material in the announcement or qualification information, **do not attach** any materials, such as: official position descriptions, performance evaluations, letters of recommendation, certificates of training, publications, etc. Any materials you attach which were not asked for may be removed from your application and will **not** be returned to you.
- We suggest that you **keep a copy** of this application for your use. If you plan to make copies of your application, we suggest you leave items **1, 48** and **49** blank. Complete these blank items each time you apply. **YOU MUST SIGN AND DATE, IN INK, EACH COPY YOU SUBMIT.**
- To apply for a specific Federal civil service examination (whether or not a written test is required) **or a specific vacancy in an Federal agency:**
  - Read the announcement and other materials provided.
  - Make sure that your work experience and/or education meet the qualification requirements described.
  - Make sure the announcement is open for the job and location you are interested in. Announcements may be closed to receipt of applications for some types of jobs, grades, or geographic locations.
  - Make sure that you are allowed to apply. Some jobs are limited to veterans, or to people who work for the Federal Government or have worked for the Federal Government in the past.
  - Follow any directions on "How to Apply." If a written test is required, bring any material you are instructed to bring to the test session. For example, you may be instructed to "Bring a completed SF 171 to the test." If a written test is not required, mail this application and all other forms required by the announcement to the address specified in the announcement.

Work Experience *(Item 24)*

- Carefully complete each experience block you need to describe your work experience. Unless you qualify based on education alone, **your rating will depend on your description of previous jobs. Do not leave out any jobs you held during the last ten years.**
- Under Description of Work, write a **clear and brief, but complete** description of your **major** duties and responsibilities for each job. Include any supervisory duties, special assignments, and your accomplishments in the job. We may verify your description with your former employers.
- If you had a major change of duties or responsibilities while you worked for the same employer, describe each major change as a separate job.

Veteran Preference in Hiring *(Item 22)*

- **DO NOT LEAVE Item 22 BLANK.** If you do **not** claim veteran preference, place an "X" in the box next to "NO PREFERENCE".
- You **cannot** receive veteran preference if you are retired or plan to retire at or above the rank of major or lieutenant commander, **unless** you are disabled or retired from the active military Reserve.
- To receive veteran preference your separation from active duty must have been under honorable conditions. This includes honorable and general discharges. A clemency discharge does not meet the requirements of the Veteran Preference Act.
- Active duty for training in the military Reserve and National Guard programs is not considered active duty for purposes of veteran preference.
- To qualify for preference you must meet ONE of the following conditions:
  1. Served on active duty anytime between December 7, 1941, and July 1, 1955; (If you were a Reservist called to active duty between February 1, 1955 and July 1, 1955, you must meet condition 2, below.)

     or
  2. Served on active duty any part of which was between July 2, 1955 and October 14, 1976 or a Reservist called to active duty between February 1, 1955 and October 14, 1976 and who served for more than 180 days;

     or
  3. Entered on active duty between October 15, 1976 and September 7, 1980 or a Reservist who entered on active duty between October 15, 1976 and October 13, 1982 **and** received a Campaign Badge or Expeditionary Medal **or** are a disabled veteran;

     or
  4. Enlisted in the Armed Forces after September 7, 1980 or entered active duty other than by enlistment on or after October 14, 1982 **and:**

     a. completed 24 months of continuous active duty or the full period called or ordered to active duty, or were discharged under 10 U.S.C. 1171 or for hardship under 10 U.S.C. 1173 **and** received or were entitled to receive a Campaign Badge or Expeditionary Medal; **or**

     b. are a disabled veteran.
- If you meet one of the four conditions above, you qualify for 5-point preference. If you want to claim 5-point preference **and** do not meet the requirements for 10-point preference, discussed below, place an "X" in the box next to "5-POINT PREFERENCE".
- If you think you qualify for 10-Point Preference, review the requirements described in the Standard Form (SF) 15, Application for 10-Point Veteran Preference. The SF 15 is available from any Federal Job Information Center. The 10-point preference groups are:
  - Non-Compensably Disabled or Purple Heart Recipient.
  - Compensably Disabled (less than 30%).
  - Compensably Disabled (30% or more).
  - Spouse, Widow(er) or Mother of a deceased or disabled veteran.
- If you claim 10-point preference, place an "X" in the box next to the group that applies to you. To receive **10-point preference you must attach a completed SF 15 to this application together with the proof requested in the SF 15.**

Privacy Act and Public Burden Statements

DETACH THIS PAGE—NOTE SF 171-A ON BACK

Application for Federal Employment—SF 171

Read the instructions before you complete this application. *Type or print clearly in dark ink.*

Form Approved
OMB No. 3206-0012

GENERAL INFORMATION

1 What kind of job are you applying for? *Give title and announcement no. (if any)*

2 Social Security Number

3 Sex
☐ Male ☐ Female

4 Birth date *(Month, Day, Year)*

5 Birthplace *(City and State or Country)*

6 Name *(Last, First, Middle)*

Mailing address *(include apartment number, if any)*

City   State   ZIP Code

7 Other names ever used *(e.g., maiden name, nickname, etc.)*

8 Home Phone
Area Code   Number

9 Work Phone
Area Code   Number   Extension

10 Were you ever employed as a civilian by the Federal Government? If **"NO"**, go to **Item 11**. If **"YES"**, mark each type of job you held with an **"X"**.

☐ Temporary ☐ Career-Conditional ☐ Career ☐ Excepted

What is your **highest** grade, classification series and job title?

Dates at **highest** grade: FROM   TO

FOR USE OF EXAMINING OFFICE ONLY

Date entered register

Form reviewed:
Form approved:

Option	Grade	Earned Rating	Veteran Preference	Augmented Rating
			☐ No Preference Claimed	
			☐ 5 Points (Tentative)	
			☐ 10 Pts. (30% Or More Comp. Dis.)	
			☐ 10 Pts. (Less Than 30% Comp. Dis.)	
			☐ Other 10 Points	

Initials and Date

☐ Disallowed ☐ Being Investigated

FOR USE OF APPOINTING OFFICE ONLY

Preference has been verified through proof that the separation was under honorable conditions, and other proof as required.

☐ 5-Point ☐ 10-Point - 30% or More Compensable Disability ☐ 10-Point - Less Than 30% Compensable Disability ☐ 10-Point - Other

Signature and Title

Agency   Date

AVAILABILITY

11 When can you start work? *(Month and Year)*

12 What is the **lowest** pay you will accept? *(You will not be considered for jobs which pay less than you indicate.)*

Pay $ _____ per _____ OR Grade _____

13 In what geographic area(s) are you willing to work?

14 Are you willing to work:

	YES	NO
A. 40 hours per week *(full-time)*?		
B. 25-32 hours per week *(part-time)*?		
C. 17-24 hours per week *(part-time)*?		
D. 16 or fewer hours per week *(part-time)*?		
E. An intermittent job *(on-call/seasonal)*?		
F. Weekends, shifts, or rotating shifts?		

15 Are you willing to take a temporary job lasting:

A. 5 to 12 months *(sometimes longer)*?
B. 1 to 4 months?
C. Less than 1 month?

16 Are you willing to travel away from home for:

A. 1 to 5 nights each month?
B. 6 to 10 nights each month?
C. 11 or more nights each month?

MILITARY SERVICE AND VETERAN PREFERENCE

17 Have you served in the United States Military Service? *If your only active duty was training in the Reserves or National Guard, answer "NO". If "NO", go to item 22.*   YES NO

18 Did you or will you retire at or above the rank of major or lieutenant commander?

THE FEDERAL GOVERNMENT IS AN EQUAL OPPORTUNITY EMPLOYER

PREVIOUS EDITION USABLE UNTIL 12-31-90

Page 1

MILITARY SERVICE AND VETERAN PREFERENCE *(Cont.)*

19 Were you discharged from the military service under honorable conditions? *(If your discharge was changed to "honorable" or "general" by a Discharge Review Board, answer "YES". If you received a clemency discharge, answer "NO".)* If "NO", provide below the date and type of discharge you received.   YES NO

Discharge Date *(Month, Day, Year)*   Type of Discharge

20 List the dates *(Month, Day, Year)*, and branch for all **active duty** military service.

From	To	Branch of Service

21 If all your active military duty was after October 14, 1976, list the full names and dates of all campaign badges or expeditionary medals you received or were entitled to receive.

22 **Read the instructions that came with this form before completing this item.** When you have determined your eligibility for veteran preference from the instructions, place an **"X"** in the box next to your veteran preference claim.

☐ NO PREFERENCE

☐ 5-POINT PREFERENCE -- You must show proof when you are hired.

☐ 10-POINT PREFERENCE -- If you claim 10-point preference, place an **"X"** in the box below next to the basis for your claim. To receive 10-point preference you must also complete a Standard Form 15, Application for 10-Point Veteran Preference, which is available from any Federal Job Information Center. ATTACH THE COMPLETED SF 15 AND REQUESTED PROOF TO THIS APPLICATION.

☐ Non-compensably disabled or Purple Heart recipient.
☐ Compensably disabled, less than 30 percent.
☐ Spouse, widow(er), or mother of a deceased or disabled veteran.
☐ Compensably disabled, 30 percent or more.

NSN 7540-00-935-7150   171-109   Standard Form 171 (Rev. 6-88)
U.S. Office of Personnel Management
FPM Chapter 295

(continued)

Figure 7 (continued)

WORK EXPERIENCE *If you have no work experience, write "NONE" in A below and go to 25 on page 3.*

23 May we ask your present employer about your character, qualifications, and work record? *A "NO" will not affect our review of your qualifications. If you answer "NO" and we need to contact your present employer before we can offer you a job, we will contact you first.* . . . . | **YES** | **NO** |

24 READ **WORK EXPERIENCE** IN THE INSTRUCTIONS BEFORE YOU BEGIN.

- Describe your current or most recent job in Block **A** and work backwards, describing each job you held **during the past 10 years.** If you were **unemployed** for longer than **3 months** within the past 10 years, list the dates and your address(es) in an experience block.

- You may sum up in one block work that you did **more than 10 years ago.** But if that work **is related** to the type of job you are applying for, describe each related job in a separate block.

- INCLUDE VOLUNTEER WORK *(non-paid work)*--**If the work** *(or a part of the work)* **is like the job you are applying for,** complete **all** parts of the experience block just as you would for a paying job. You may receive credit for work experience with religious, community, welfare, service, and other organizations.

- INCLUDE MILITARY SERVICE--You should complete **all** parts of the experience block just as you would for a non-military job, including **all** supervisory experience. Describe each major change of duties or responsibilities in a separate experience block.

- IF YOU NEED MORE SPACE TO DESCRIBE A JOB--Use sheets of paper the same size as this page (be sure to include **all** information we ask for in **A** and **B** below). On **each** sheet show your name, Social Security Number, and the announcement number or job title.

- IF YOU NEED MORE EXPERIENCE BLOCKS, use the SF 171-A or a sheet of paper.

- IF YOU NEED TO UPDATE (ADD MORE RECENT JOBS), use the SF 172 or a sheet of paper as described above.

A | Name and address of employer's organization *(include ZIP Code, if known)* | Dates employed *(give month, day and year)* From: To: | Average number if hours per week | Number of employees you supervise |

Salary or earnings
Starting $ per
Ending $ per | Your reason for wanting to leave

Your immediate supervisor
Name   Area Code   Telephone No.   Exact title of your job   If Federal employment *(civilian or military)* list series, grade or rank, and, if promoted in this job, the date of your last promotion

Description of work: Describe your specific duties, responsibilities and accomplishments in this job, **including** the job title(s) of any employees you supervise. *If you describe more than one type of work (for example, carpentry and painting, or personnel and budget), write the approximate percentage of time you spent doing each.*

For Agency Use (skill codes. etc.)

B | Name and address of employer's organization *(include ZIP Code, if known)* | Dates employed *(give month, day and year)* From: To: | Average number of hours per week | Number of employees you supervised |

Salary or earnings
Starting $ per
Ending $ per | Your reason for leaving

Your immediate supervisor
Name   Area Code   Telephone No.   Exact title of your job   If Federal employment *(civilian or military)* list series, grade or rank, and, if promoted in this job, the date of your last promotion

Description of work: Describe your specific duties, responsibilities and accomplishments in this job, **including** the job title(s) of any employees you supervised. *If you describe more than one type of work (for example, carpentry and painting, or personnel and budget), write the approximate percentage of time you spent doing each.*

For Agency Use (skill codes. etc.)

Page 2   IF YOU NEED MORE EXPERIENCE BLOCKS, USE SF 171-A *(SEE BACK OF INSTRUCTION PAGE).*

— ◄——————— **ATTACH ANY ADDITIONAL FORMS AND SHEETS HERE**

EDUCATION

25 Did you graduate from high school? *If you have a GED high school equivalency or will graduate within the next nine months, answer "YES".*

YES ▶	If "YES", give month and year graduated or received GED equivalency:...............
NO ▶	If "NO", give the highest grade you completed:...........

26 Write the name and location *(city and state)* of the last high school you attended or where you obtained your GED high school equivalency.

27 Have you ever attended college or graduate school? **YES** ▶ If "YES", continue with **28**. **NO** ▶ If "NO", go to **31**.

28 NAME AND LOCATION *(city, state and ZIP Code)* OF COLLEGE OR UNIVERSITY. *If you expect to graduate within nine months, give the* **month** *and* **year** *you expect to receive your degree:*

Name	City	State	ZIP Code	MONTH AND YEAR ATTENDED From	To	NUMBER OF CREDIT HOURS COMPLETED Semester	Quarter	TYPE OF DEGREE *(e.g. B.A., M.A.)*	MONTH AND YEAR OF DEGREE
1)									
2)									
3)									

29 CHIEF UNDERGRADUATE SUBJECTS *Show major on the first line*

	NUMBER OF CREDIT HOURS COMPLETED Semester	Quarter
1)		
2)		
3)		

30 CHIEF GRADUATE SUBJECTS *Show major on the first line*

	NUMBER OF CREDIT HOURS COMPLETED Semester	Quarter
1)		
2)		
3)		

31 If you have completed any **other courses or training related to the kind of jobs you are applying** for *(trade, vocational, Armed Forces, business)* give information below.

NAME AND LOCATION *(city, state and ZIP Code)* OF SCHOOL	MONTH AND YEAR ATTENDED From	To	CLASS-ROOM HOURS	SUBJECT(S)	TRAINING COMPLETED YES	NO
School Name 1)						
City State ZIP Code						
School Name 2)						
City State ZIP Code						

SPECIAL SKILLS, ACCOMPLISHMENTS AND AWARDS

32 Give the title and year of any honors, awards or fellowships you have received. List your special qualifications, skills or accomplishments that may help you get a job. *Some examples are: skills with computers or other machines; most important publications (do not submit copies); public speaking and writing experience; membership in professional or scientific societies; patents or inventions; etc.*

33 How many words per minute can you: TYPE? TAKE DICTATION? *Agencies may test your skills before hiring you.*

34 List **job-related** licenses or certificates that you have, such as: *registered nurse; lawyer; radio operator; driver's; pilot's; etc.*

	LICENSE OR CERTIFICATE	DATE OF LATEST LICENSE OR CERTIFICATE	STATE OR OTHER LICENSING AGENCY
1)			
2)			

35 Do you speak or read a language other than English *(include sign language)?* **Applicants for jobs that require a language other than English may be given an interview conducted solely in that language.** **YES** ▶ If "YES", list each language and place an "X" in each column that applies to you. **NO** ▶ If "NO", go to **36**.

LANGUAGE(S)	CAN PREPARE AND GIVE LECTURES Fluently	With Difficulty	CAN SPEAK AND UNDERSTAND Fluently	Passably	CAN TRANSLATE ARTICLES Into English	From English	CAN READ ARTICLES FOR OWN USE Easily	With Difficulty
1)								
2)								

REFERENCES

36 List three people who are not related to you and are not supervisors you listed under **24** who know your qualifications and fitness for the kind of job for which you are applying. At least **one** should know you well on a personal basis.

FULL NAME OF REFERENCE	TELEPHONE NUMBER(S) *(Include Area Code)*	PRESENT BUSINESS OR HOME ADDRESS *(Number, street and city)*	STATE	ZIP CODE
1)				
2)				
3)				

Page 3

(continued)

Figure 7 *(continued)*

BACKGROUND INFORMATION--*You must answer each question in this section before we can process your application.*

37 Are you a citizen of the United States? *(In most cases you must be a U.S. citizen to be hired. You will be required to submit proof of identity and citizenship at the time you are hired.)* If "NO", give the country or countries you are a citizen of: _____ | **YES** | **NO** |

NOTE: It is important that you give complete and truthful answers to questions 38 through 44. If you answer "YES" to any of them, provide your explanation(s) in **Item 45**. **Include** convictions resulting from a plea of nolo contendere *(no contest).* **Omit:** 1) traffic fines of $100.00 or less; 2) any violation of law committed before your 16th birthday; 3) any violation of law committed before your 18th birthday, if finally decided in juvenile court or under a Youth Offender law; 4) any conviction set aside under the Federal Youth Corrections Act or similar State law; 5) any conviction whose record was expunged under Federal or State law. We will consider the date, facts, and circumstances of each event you list. In most cases you can still be considered for Federal jobs. However, **if you fail to tell the truth or fail to list all relevant** events or circumstances, this may be grounds for not hiring you, for firing you after you begin work, or for criminal prosecution (18 USC 1001).

38 During the last **10 years**, were you **fired from any job** for any reason, did you **quit after being told that you would be fired**, or did you leave by mutual agreement because of specific problems?. . . . . | **YES** | **NO** |

39 Have you **ever** been convicted of, or forfeited collateral for **any felony violation**? *(Generally, a felony is defined as any violation of law punishable by imprisonment of longer than one year, except for violations called misdemeanors under State law which are punishable by imprisonment of two years or less.)* . . . .

40 Have you **ever** been convicted of, or forfeited collateral for **any firearms or explosives violation**? . . . .

41 Are you **now** under charges for **any** violation of law? . . . .

42 During the **last 10 years** have you forfeited collateral, been convicted, been imprisoned, been on probation, or been on parole? Do **not** include violations reported in 39, 40, or 41, above. . . . .

43 Have you **ever** been convicted by a military **court-martial**? If no military service, answer "NO". . . . .

44 Are you **delinquent** on any Federal debt? *(Include delinquencies arising from Federal taxes, loans, overpayment of benefits, and other debts to the U.S. Government **plus** defaults on Federally guaranteed or insured loans such as student and home mortgage loans.)* . . . .

45 If "YES" in: 38 - Explain for each job the problem(s) and your reason(s) for leaving. Give the employer's name and address.
   39 through 43 - Explain each violation. Give place of occurrence and name/address of police or court involved.
      44 - Explain the type, length and amount of the delinquency or default, and steps you are taking to correct errors or repay the debt. Give any identification number associated with the debt and the address of the Federal agency involved.
   NOTE: If you need more space, use a sheet of paper, and include the item number.

Item No.	Date (Mo./Yr.)	Explanation	Mailing Address
			Name of Employer, Police, Court, or Federal Agency
			City / State / ZIP Code
			Name of Employer, Police, Court, or Federal Agency
			City / State / ZIP Code

46 Do you receive, or have you ever applied for retirement pay, pension, or other pay based on military, Federal civilian, or District of Columbia Government service? . . . . | **YES** | **NO** |

47 Do any of your relatives work for the United States Government or the United States Armed Forces? Include: *father; mother; husband; wife; son; daughter; brother; sister; uncle; aunt; first cousin; nephew; niece; father-in-law; mother-in-law; son-in-law; daughter-in-law; brother-in-law; sister-in-law; stepfather; stepmother; stepson; stepdaughter; stepbrother; stepsister; half brother; and half sister.* . . . .
If "YES", provide details below. If you need more space, use a sheet of paper.

Name	Relationship	Department, Agency or Branch of Armed Forces

SIGNATURE, CERTIFICATION, AND RELEASE OF INFORMATION

YOU MUST SIGN THIS APPLICATION. Read the following carefully before you sign.

- A false statement on any part of your application may be grounds for not hiring you, or for firing you after you begin work. Also, you may be punished by fine or imprisonment (U.S. Code, title 18, section 1001).
- If you are a male born after December 31, 1959 you must be registered with the Selective Service System or have a valid exemption in order to be eligible for Federal employment. You will be required to certify as to your status at the time of appointment.
- I **understand** that any information I give may be investigated as allowed by law or Presidential order.
- I **consent** to the release of information about my ability and fitness for Federal employment by *employers, schools, law enforcement agencies and other individuals and organizations,* to *investigators, personnel staffing specialists, and other authorized employees of the Federal Government.*
- I **certify** that, to the best of my knowledge and belief, **all** of my statements are true, correct, complete, and made in good faith.

48 SIGNATURE *(Sign each application in dark ink)* | **49** DATE SIGNED *(Month, day, year)*

*U.S. Government Printing Office: 1989-241-175/80274

Standard Form 171-A— *Continuation Sheet for SF 171*

Form Approved
OMB No. 3206-0012

• Attach all SF 171-A's to your application at the top of page 3.

1. Name *(Last, First, Middle Initial)*	2. Social Security Number

3. Job Title or Announcement Number You Are Applying For	4. Date Completed

ADDITIONAL WORK EXPERIENCE BLOCKS

Name and address of employer's organization *(include ZIP Code, if known)*	Dates employed *(give month, day and year)*	Average number of hours per week	Number of employees you supervised
	From: To:		
	Salary or earnings	Your reason for leaving	
	Starting $ per		
	Ending $ per		

Your immediate supervisor		Exact title of your job	If Federal employment *(civilian or military)* list series, grade or rank, and, if promoted in this job, the date of your last promotion
Name	Area Code Telephone No.		

Description of work: Describe your specific duties, responsibilities and accomplishments in this job, **including** the job title(s) of any employees you supervised. *If you describe more than one type of work (for example, carpentry and painting, or personnel and budget), write the approximate percentage of time you spent doing each.*

For Agency Use (skill codes, etc.)

Name and address of employer's organization *(include ZIP Code, if known)*	Dates employed *(give month, day and year)*	Average number of hours per week	Number of employees you supervised
	From: To:		
	Salary or earnings	Your reason for leaving	
	Starting $ per		
	Ending $ per		

Your immediate supervisor		Exact title of your job	If Federal employment *(civilian or military)* list series, grade or rank, and, if promoted in this job, the date of your last promotion
Name	Area Code Telephone No.		

Description of work: Describe your specific duties, responsibilities and accomplishments in this job, **including** the job title(s) of any employees you supervised. *If you describe more than one type of work (for example, carpentry and painting, or personnel and budget), write the approximate percentage of time you spent doing each.*

For Agency Use (skill codes, etc.)

THE FEDERAL GOVERNMENT IS AN EQUAL OPPORTUNITY EMPLOYER
PREVIOUS EDITION USABLE

Standard Form 171-A (Rev. 6-88)
U.S. Office of Personnel Management
FPM Chapter 295

at each grade level for many federal jobs. Occupations are listed in series of numbers and the closer the numbers, the more similar the positions. Includes: occupational information, titles, classification factors, qualifications required, and different grade levels available for that occupation. Available at Federal Job Information Centers, federal personnel offices, and selected university and local libraries.

Section 32   This section for special skills, accomplishments, and awards, is an opportunity for you to elaborate on your qualifications. It is a small space and usually warrants including an attachment. You can include and list the following information: proficiency with software programs and hardware under skills with computers; publications, whether published or not, including handbooks, training manuals, and newsletters, for paid and nonpaid experience; public speaking and writing experience including keynote speaker, speeches, training programs and articles, columns, speeches; any professional memberships; awards and honors including special increases, cash bonuses, letters of commendation, and letters of appreciation.

KSAOs   Knowledge, Skills, Abilities, and Other Characteristics (KSAOs) are special rating factors described on vacancy announcements that are the basis of the applicant's rating. There is no standard practice regarding these factors. Some agencies require submission of special forms, while others accept applicant prepared forms. Some agencies require no additional forms but the KSAOs must be addressed on the SF-171. Check with each agency for their requirements.

X-118 Handbook   Provides current qualification standards for various grade level occupations in the federal government. Includes description of work experience requirements, specialized experience, quality of experience, personal characteristics, basis of rating, and suggestions for evaluating candidates. Available at Federal Job Information Centers, federal personnel offices, and selected university and local libraries.

Ten Steps to Completing an Effective SF-171

1. Pay attention to form and content. Form is the organization, layout, and overall appearance while content is what you say and how you present your qualifications.

2. Write the experience sections so they are easy to read. Include key information in short, direct sentences, using the active voice. Avoid pronouns, acronyms, and stilted, unnatural language. Organize your information in several paragraphs or use identations or bullets. Don't waste space with lengthy descriptions of your organization. A short description will do.

3. Focus on accomplishments, achievements, and contributions. How did you handle problems and what were the results? Quantify

wherever possible. Include honors and commendations in applicable experience sections as well as Section 32.

4. Convey skills, knowledge, and ability for all qualifications listed on a job announcement. Expand on any experience, education, training, self-development, and awards and commendations that you have that relate to the job requirements.

5. Create attachments for any section with extensive information. This gives a better overall appearance. On a plain sheet of paper use a heading, Attachment 1, and cross-reference in applicable section, "See Attachment 1."

6. An attachment for section 32 may include separate subheadings for special qualification or skills, such as computer skills; public speaking such as speeches, training, or presentations; writing experience such as published and unpublished handbooks, manuals, articles, newsletters, and books.

7. Be consistent in type, presentation, style, and format. When you update your SF-171, use the same type and format.

8. Check and recheck your grammar, punctuation, and spelling. Avoid redundancies. There is a tendency to overuse the expressions "responsible for" and "worked with." substitute "fully accountable" or "interacted with."

9. Expanded SF-171 forms are available from private sources (see below). They're typeset SF-171 forms that don't have any lines (so they look better and they're easier to type) and they come with one experience section on a page, two on a page, and three on a page.

10. Prepare an original SF-171 and make clean copies. Do not sign the original. Sign, date, and submit a copy.

SF-171 Aids

Excellent books and software are available to guide you through the writing and producing process. The following section contains the best of them.

Books

How to Find a Federal Job
Krandall Kraus
Facts on File, Inc.
460 Park Ave. S
New York, NY 10016
(212) 683-2244
Walks you through the federal job search process. Extensive information on how to find a federal job and write an effective SF-171. 1986.

The Complete Guide to Public Employment
Ronald L. Krannich &
Caryl Rae Krannich
Impact Publications
4580 Sunshine Ct.
Woodbridge, VA 22192
(703) 361-7300

Comprehensive overview and strategies to identify opportunities in state, local, and federal government; Capitol Hill and Judiciary; contractors and consultants; trade and professional associations, nonprofit organizations, foundation and research organizations; political support, influence, and management groups. Numerous resources. 1989.

The 171 Reference Book
Patricia Wood
Workbooks, Inc.
Box 4955
Timonium, MD 21093
(301) 561-8789

One of the best references for writing a SF-171. Well-organized, easy to follow, and excellent examples. Also available are Expanded 171 forms, typeset forms with more room for experience sections and *The 171 Writing Portfolio*, a 24-page excerpt from the above book and expanded 171 forms. 1986.

Computer Software

Federal Job Link
Multisoft Resources
Box 235
Washington Grove, MD
20880-0235
(301) 977-6972

Program for completing and printing SF-171 for the MacIntosh computer. Easily produces well-organized application using modified pages with the ability to customize applications and target for specific jobs. Prints forms

and answers in one step. Includes 20-page reference guide describing Federal employment process, tips, and approaches to composing application. Requires MacDraw I and II version and an Imagewriter or LaserWriter printer. 1988.

Federal Occupational and Career Information System (FOCIS)
NTIS
5285 Port Royal Rd.
Springfield, VA 22161
(703) 487-4650

Excellent program assisting the white-collar job seeker in identifying interests and learning about job opportunities in the Executive Branch of the federal government. Identifies opportunities by over 100 college majors and lists up to 10 specific occupations for each major. Lists job descriptions, minimum qualifications required, grades and salary information, agencies that hire the occupation and where located, and number currently employed for 360 occupations. Alphabetical list of hiring agencies, by subdivisions, regions, states, and cities, providing agency descriptions and addresses. Can print information by screen, not file, using print screen key. Systems requirements include IBM PC or compatible with a high density (1.2 megabyte) 5¼-inch disk drive. 1990.

Quick & Easy for the SF-171
DataTech
4820 Derry St.
Harrisburg, PA 17111
(717) 561-1335

Program for completing and printing SF-171 for IBM PC available in Personal Version (one person), Family Pack (two people), or Office Pack (eight people). Write your SF-171 prior to beginning program. Allows user to create unlimited number of 171 files. Spelling checker with a 112,000-word dic-

tionary. Several print options. Printing a facsimile with a laser printer requires 1.5 megabyte of memory. 1991.

Expanded SF-171 Forms

Expanded SF-171 forms are available from:

Federal Research Service, Inc.
243 Church St. NW
Box 1059
Vienna, VA 22183-1059
(202) 333-5627; (800) 822-JOBS

Workbooks, Inc.
Box 4955
Timonium, MD 21093
(301) 561-8789

Cover Letters That Catch Attention

Your résumé or SF-171 should always be accompanied by a cover letter. It introduces you to the reader and entices him or her to read your résumé or SF-171. Written communication skills are highly desirable and a well-written letter and résumé are your best chances of making it to the next step in the hiring process, the job interview.

If you follow these tips you'll write a letter that will catch the reader's attention and get results.

- The cover letter should be one-page long and consist of five to six paragraphs. Full-block and semiblock paragraphs are appropriate for business formats.
- Avoid beginning the letter and other paragraphs with the pronoun *I* (Instead, open with a strong statement about the organization or the career field. Use statistics, information from a journal or magazine article, or facts you have uncovered in research.

   For example: *Business Magazine* describes your company as a dynamic leader in the field of office products. To maintain your leadership position, competitive product pricing and effective customer service are paramount.
- State brief facts about your experience and accomplishments in the middle of the letter. Use some facts not included in your resume or SF-171 such as specific skills, accomplishments, or a summary of your unique contributions.
- Keep the tone positive and upbeat. End your letter requesting an interview or with a statement that you will call to arrange one.

(*text continues on page 128*)

Figure 8. Sample cover letter with opening statement.

August 23, 1991

ABC Shipping
56 Main Street
Greensboro, NC 27412

Dear Mr. Adams:

The financial areas benefit from computer expertise through more efficient operations, cost effectiveness, and greater accuracy.
My experience has developed computer skills in:

• Mainframe applications
• PC software
• Data management
• Management Information Systems

Most recently these skills have been used in a consolidated corporation developing and implementing a new Management Information System.

My previous experience incorporates handling all accounting functions within the finance division. The enclosed résumé highlights my experience and accomplishments.

I will be relocating to Greensboro in October and plan on being in the area the week of September 10th. I would like to meet with you and discuss opportunities in your organization and will call you to schedule an appointment.

I look forward to speaking with you.

Sincerely yours,

Beth Sperry

Encl.

Figure 9. Sample cover letter without opening statement.

March 19, 1994

National Builders' Corp.
4 Main Street
Las Vegas, Nevada 89104

Dear Mr. Elden:

With more than 10 years' experience in the customer service field, my experience duplicates your requirements for a Customer Service Manager.

My expertise is in the initiation and implementation of customer care programs. I have recently successfully integrated sales and customer service support for a multinational corporation.

Last year, under my direction, my organization achieved the highest regional award for customer satisfaction. The enclosed résumé outlines my experience and contributions.

I can contribute to your organization's effectiveness by establishing good working relations with customers and personnel at all organizational levels.

I am eager to learn more about the Customer Service Manager position and would like to discuss my qualifications and interests with you.

Thanks for your time and consideration.

Sincerely,

Roger Small

enc.

- Use the same paper for both your letter and résumé. Type each letter individually using a correcting electric typewriter, word processor, or word processing software (see Figures 8 and 9).

Resources

The following resources will help you write an effective cover letter.

Books

Dynamic Cover Letters
Katharine Hansen with
   Randall Hansen
Ten Speed Press
Box 7123
Berkeley, CA 94707
(415) 845-8414
An excellent guide that covers writing, mechanics, editing, numerous examples, as well an many inside tips to get your cover letter and résumé read. Highly recommended. 1990.

200 Letters for Job Hunters
William S. Frank
   Ten Speed Press
   [see above]
One of the best books available on cover letters. Wonderful examples of every type of letter you'll use during the job search. 1990.

Computer Software

INSTANT Job Hunting Letters
CareerLab
7700 E. Arapahoe Rd., Ste. 275
Englewood, CO 80112-9981
(303) 771-4357
Based on William Frank's book, *200 Letter for Job Hunters,* features 200 letters aimed to get you results. For the IBM PC and compatibles. Requires a word processing program and letter quality printer.

Chapter 8

Looking for Leads
in All the Right Places

If you are using just the Sunday employment classified section of your newspaper to search for job opportunities, you are missing out on 90 percent of the job openings. A comprehensive survey of the job seeking methods of 10.4 million men and women, done in 1973 but still considered valid, by the U.S. Department of Labor, Bureau of Labor Statistics, indicates that not only are only 10 percent of all jobs found through the employment classified section, but 50 percent of all job seekers prefer this method for securing jobs. That means you'll be competing with 50 percent of the people for 10 percent of the jobs.

A more current survey of job seeking methods was conducted in 1989 by the Erdlen Bograd Group, an outplacement firm in Wellesley, Massachusetts.

How Job Seekers Find Jobs	
Networking	34.1%
Advertising	23.4
Employment agencies	17.1
Direct contact	6.2
Executive search consultants	4.6
Job fairs	2.7
Miscellaneous	11.9
Total	100.0%

While it is important for you to know how other people find jobs, it's perhaps even more telling to understand how employers find employees. The Erdlen Bograd Group also conducted a national survey in 1989 of a broad range of organizations, large and small, to learn just that. What follows are the results.

How Companies Hire	
Employee referrals	38.2%
Advertising	22.1
Employment agencies	19.6
Direct contact	6.4
Executive search firms	1.8
Miscellaneous	12.9
Total	100.0%

*Includes open houses, job fairs, out-placement firms, and associations.

Many job seekers use traditional options such as employment classified advertising, federal and state employment services, employment agencies, and executive recruiters. While these can be effective means for finding job opportunities, you can increase your odds for success by using a wide variety of sources available to you including nontraditional methods such as job listing periodicals, journals and magazines, on-line career information sources, job banks, dial-a-job, local colleges and universities, in-house opportunities, and job fairs.

Employment Classified Advertising

You might think it would be easy to hook up with job openings using the classified ads; after all, these companies are looking for employees, aren't they? Well, some of them are and some of them aren't. And even if they are, how will you catch their attention when so many other job seekers are competing for the same openings?

First, we'll address the fact that all jobs advertised in the classified section don't exist or aren't available. Employers who do business with the federal government must advertise their jobs to comply with regulations. In compliance, many of these jobs are advertised, even though the organization has already selected someone to fill the position. Some ads request salary requirements and organizations use this information to revamp their salary scales, while others are run by employment agencies to add future candidates to their files.

If you plan to use the classified ads, prepare to compete effectively with the competition—there will be plenty of it. An ad run by a large company in the Sunday edition of the *Washington Post* employment classified section can easily attract 1,000 to 2,000 résumés the first five days. How will your résumé stand out in that crowd?

Begin by reading the entire employment section. Jobs that match your interests and qualifications might appear anywhere from A to Z. Circle jobs of interest with a felt pen highlighter.

Write personal, effective cover letters for all the jobs and send these with a good copy of your résumé. If no contact is indicated, begin your letter with "Dear Employer" or, if an organization and job title are given, call the organization directly and ask for the name of the individual holding the job title.

You want your letter and résumé to be at the head of the pack so get your letters mailed first thing Sunday or early Monday.

Employment Agencies

Employment agencies are private companies that place secretarial, clerical, word processing, administrative, and office support staff usually paying annual salaries of $15,000 to $45,000.

You'll find agencies that specialize in professions and industries (for example, paralegal, accounting, food service, hospitality, medical/dental, data processing, sales, editorial, insurance, and banking). Check the Yellow Pages of your phone directory or the newspaper employment classified section.

Simply working with an agency is not the only way a job seeker should go and even though I'm in the business I would say do your own direct mail campaigns, use us as an extra source, network on your own, go after everything that you can. I wouldn't count totally on an employment service. I would visit a couple of them, too, see what everyone has to offer.

Nancy Schuman,
Vice President,
Marketing and Operation,
Career Blazers Personnel Services

Employment agencies work on a contingency basis, earning a fee when they successfully place a candidate with a client. The hiring company (the client) usually pays the fee. Check fee arrangements and terms prior to working with an employment agency.

You can locate agencies through referrals from colleagues and friends, listings in the Sunday newspaper employment classified section, and the Yellow Pages of the phone directory.

The following resource provides a national membership listing of the National Association of Personnel Consultants:

National Directory of Personnel Consultants
National Association of Personnel Consultants
3133 Mt. Vernon Ave.
Alexandria, VA 22305
(703) 684-0180
Lists 2,200 executive recruiters, placement firms, and employment agencies that are members of their organization, located throughout the United States, by geographical area and specializations. Includes Index of Job Titles/Job Descriptions. 1990.

Executive Recruiters

Executive recruiters place professionals in a wide range of fields and careers, usually paying annual salaries of $30,000 and up. Executive search firms, sometimes referred to as headhunters, place senior executive level positions paying annual salaries of $80,000 and up.

These firms work on a contingency or retainer basis. Locate them through referrals from colleagues and friends and listings in the Sunday newspaper employment classified section and the Yellow Pages of the phone directory.

The following directory lists executive recruiters and executive search firms.

Directory of Executive Recruiters
Kennedy Publications
Templeton Rd.
Fitzwilliam, NH 03447
(603) 585-2200
Lists and describes more than 2,100 firms in more than 3,900 offices in North America. Cross-indexed by function/industry/geography. Contains a 100-page introduction to the executive search and how it affects job candidates and explains the importance of professional affiliations in this field. 1990.

Federal and State Employment Services

Most states have employment agencies or commissions to help unemployed workers find jobs. They offer different services from job listings, job banks, counseling, and job fairs. Information about jobs in other states may be available. Find your local office by checking in the government listings in your phone directory.

Job Listing Periodicals

Job listing periodicals, available by subscription, carry listings of job vacancies for different career fields. The following are periodicals, organized by career and industry.

Business

The National Ad Search
Box 2083
Milwaukee, WI 53201
(414) 351-1398; (800) 992-2832
Weekly periodical, approximately 84 pages, containing 2,000 new jobs in more than 50 categorized areas of expertise; compilation of 75 major newspapers throughout the United States. Includes professional, executive, technical, and managerial.

National Business Employment
Weekly
Dow Jones and Co., Inc.
Box 300
Princeton, NJ 08540
(609) 520-4000
Weekly newspaper that includes employment listings from the regional editions of *The Wall Street Journal*.

Computers

PD News
12416 Hymeadow Dr.
Austin, TX 78750
(512) 250-8127; (800) 678-9724
Weekly job listing (Captsule), arranged geographically, for contract computer employees.

Criminal Justice

NELS (National Employment
Listing Service) Bulletin
Criminal Justice Center
Sam Houston State Univ.
Huntsville, TX 77341-2296
(409) 294-1692/90
Monthly listing of national positions in law enforcement and security, institutional corrections, community services, academics and research, and court administration.

Economics

Job Openings for Economists
American Economics Association
1313 21st Ave.
Suite 809
Nashville, TN 37212

Education

Chronicle of Higher Education
1255 23rd St.
Suite 700
Washington, DC 20037
Weekly publication listing national academic job opportunities.

MLA Job Information List
10 Astor Pl.
New York, NY 10003-6981
(212) 614-6384
Quarterly publication listing teaching positions in colleges and universities in English, foreign languages, comparative literature, and linguistics.

National Education Service Center
Box 1279
Riverton, WY 82501-1279
(307) 856-0170
Weekly newsletter lists job opportunities for teachers, administrators, and education specialists in private and public schools at the elementary, secondary, and postsecondary levels.

Environment

Environmental Opportunities
Box 4957
Arcata,CA 95521
(707) 839-4640
Monthly bulletin listing national entry- and mid-level environmental jobs primarily in the private sector. Includes teaching, administration, horticulture, outdoor education, fisheries, biology, ecology, wildlife, nature center, research, organizational, seasonal positions, and internships.

International

International Employment Hotline
WorldWise Books
Box 3030
Oakton, VA 22124-9030
Monthly newsletter listing worldwide job openings organized by country.

Health

See *The National Ad Search* under business in this chapter.

Legal

Job Announcements
National Center for State Courts
300 Newport Ave.
Williamsburg, VA 23187-8798
(804) 253-2000
Biweekly publication listing national job opportunities for legal and judicial personnel.

National and Federal Legal Employment Report
Federal Reports
1010 Vermont Ave. NW
Ste. 408
Washington, DC 20005
(202) 393-3311
Monthly, detailed listing, available by subscription, of attorney- and law-related job opportunities in the federal government and public/private employers throughout the United States and abroad.

Librarianship

See *The City-County Recruiter and The State Recruiter* under Public Sector in this chapter.

Nonprofit

Community Jobs
1516 P St. NW
Washington, DC 20005
(202) 667-0661

Monthly detailed listing, available by subscription, of national jobs and internships in nonprofit, community, social change, and socially responsible organizations.

Planning

JobMart
American Planning Association
1313 E. 60th St.
Chicago, IL 60637
(312) 955-9100

Job service with listings in planning and zoning, economic development, housing, transportation, environmental management, urban design, historic preservation, and grants administration in government, private sector, and universities. Mailed twenty-two times a year.

See *The City-County Recruiter and The State Recruiter* listed under Public Sector in this chapter.

Public Sector

The City-County Recruiter and The State Recruiter
Box 2400, Station B
Lincoln, NE 68502
(402) 476-9120

A biweekly listing of job opportunities within city, county, and state government agencies. Includes administrative/management, engineering/transportation, library science, planning/community development, police/criminal justice.

Federal Career Opportunities
Federal Research Service
Box 1059, Ste. 5
Vienna, VA 22183-1059
(202) FED-JOBS; (800) 822-JOBS

Biweekly listing, available by subscription, of national and overseas federal job opportunities.

Federal Jobs Digest
Box 594
Millwood, NY 10546-9989
(800) 824-5000 (order line)

Bimonthly publication listing national federal openings for all professions and occupations including senior executive service and Capitol Hill jobs.

Federal Times
6883 Commercial Dr.
Springfield, VA 22159-0260
(703) 750-8600

Weekly publication listing national and international federal civil service jobs, GS-7s or above, as well as senior executive service.

The Job Finder
Western Governmental Research Association
c/o Graduate Center of Public Policy and Administration
California State Univ., Long Beach
1250 Bellflower Blvd.
Long Beach, CA 90840
(213) 985-5419

Monthly listing of job openings in public administration and governmental research in thirteen Western states.

Psychology

The APA Monitor
1200 17th St. NW

Washington, DC 20036
(202) 955-7600

Monthly newspaper of the American Psychological Association. Lists national and international job openings for psychologists.

Public Affairs

Opportunities in Public Affairs
The Brubach Corp.
1100 Connecticut Ave., Ste. 700
Washington, DC 20036
(202) 861-0590

Biweekly publication listing national public affairs openings in the public and private sectors.

Public Relations/ Communications

The Placement Service
Philadelphia Public Relations
   Society
Contact: Dr. Jean Brodey
Dept. of Journalism
Temple Univ.
Philadelphia, PA 19122
(215) 787-8757

Placement Service Newsletter sponsored by the Philadelphia Chapter of the Public Relations Society of America. Published eleven times a year for positions mostly in Mid-Atlantic area.

PR MARCOM JOBS WEST
Rachel P. R. Services
513 Wilshire Blvd., Ste. 238
Santa Monica, CA 90401
(213) 326-2661; (213) 395-7678

Bimonthly listing of West Coast corporate, agency, and nonprofit job opportunities in advertising, public relations, and marketing.

Social Service

Social Service Jobs
Employment Listing for the
   Social Services
10 Angelica Dr.
Framingham, MA 01701

Biweekly newsletter of national job openings for social workers, counselors, psychologists, and administrators in public and private agencies and organizations.

Sociology

ASA Employment Bulletin
American Sociological Association
1722 N St. NW
Washington, DC 20036
(202) 833-3410

Monthly listing of positions in academia, professors, chairs, and research; applied in research inside and outside institutions; fellowships in institutions and organizations.

Telecommunications

See *The National Ad Search* under *Business* in this chapter.
   Research additional newsletters by checking the following annual directories under *Careers, Employment,* or by industry name.

The Standard Periodical Directory
Oxbridge Communications
150 Fifth Ave.
New York, NY 10011
(212) 741-0231

Directory of Publications
Gale Research Co.
835 Penobscot Bldg.
Detroit, MI 48226
(313) 961-2242; (800) 347-GALE

Ulrich's International Periodicals Directory
R. R. Bowker
245 W. 17th St.
New York, NY 10011
(800) 346-6049

Journals/Magazines

Thousands of job openings are advertised in professional journals and magazines. These publications include articles, resources, and information usually directed at specific occupations and are published by magazine publishers and trade and professional associations.

The following directories cite periodicals that list job vacancy announcements in hundreds of fields. They contain comprehensive indexes that will help you locate the journals and magazines most likely to help you uncover leads.

*The Professional and Trade
  Association Job Finder*
S. Norman Feingold &
  Avis Nicholson
Garrett Park Press
Garrett Park, MD 20896
(301) 946-2553
Directory of over 1,000 groups that help job seekers learn about careers and find positions. Contains occupation grid indexing groups by career fields. 1983.

*Where the Jobs Are:
  A Comprehensive Directory
  of 1200 Journals Listing
  Career Opportunities*
S. Norman Feingold &
  Glenda Ann Hansard-Winkler
Garrett Park Press
[*see above*]
This is the updated and expanded version of *900,000 Plus Jobs Annually: Published Sources of Employment Listings*. Lists where jobs are advertised in hundreds of career fields. Extensive directory of magazines and comprehensive index to locate periodicals. 1989.

The following directory is a descriptive guide to journals, magazines, bulletins, and other publications issued by associations, societies, institutes, and other nonprofit membership organizations.

Association Periodicals Encyclopedia of Associations Series
Gale Research Co.
835 Penobscot Bldg.
Detroit, MI 48226
(313) 961-2242; (800) 347-GALE

Directory divided by (1) business, finance, industry, trade; (2) science, medicine, technology; (3) social sciences, education, humanities. Includes cumulative title, key word, and association indexes. Updated annually.

On-Line Career Information Sources

You can use your computer to post your résumé with employment registries and locate jobs through on-line utilities, information services, and public and private electronic bulletin board systems.

Terms You Need to Know

BBS An electronic bulletin board system (BBS) is an online system requiring a computer, modem, telephone connection, and communications software. The BBS allows users at remote locations to make and receive calls to the host (BBS) computer. You can post and receive messages, like a traditional bulletin board, as well as obtain information by downloading files.

on-line information services Commerical systems providing access to databases, information services, and special interest groups.

downloading Transferring information via computer from the BBS or on-line information services to your computer using your modem and communications software.

uploading Transferring information from your computer to the BBS or on-line information services or other computer systems using your modem and communications software.

modem A hardware device that changes outgoing computer signals into sound and incoming sound into computer signals. This device lets computers talk to each other.

communications software Software programs that make it possible to connect your computer to other computers through telephone lines.

electronic mail (E-Mail) Sending and receiving messages to others via the computer.

sysop The person who sets up and runs a BBS.

conference (or forum) A special area of a BBS dedicated to a specific subject or topic such as careers or employment.

To access systems, you'll need a personal computer, a modem, communications software, and a telephone line.

On-line, or information utilities and information services operate on large computer systems allowing many users to simultaneously access the system. These services sell or exchange information on a wide variety of subjects. Commercial services require the subscriber to register and pay an initial fee. Costs for accessing the system vary, depending on the time of the call and length of connect time. Subscribers access these systems by dialing a toll free or local number.

Job seekers will find commercial on-line information services useful in several ways. Some services have job listings and information on career and employment related issues. If you find a job of interest, you can reply by mail or electronically via your computer. E-mail service can be used to communicate with prospective employers to answer job listings or to obtain company information.

The electronic BBS is a medium for sharing information, in this case, among computer users. You can leave public or private messages in BBS areas, called conferences or forums, that are organized by topic or subject. Many private bulletin boards are operated by local computer user groups, search firms, corporations, and private individuals. Fees are usually nominal, if not free. Donations and subscription rate amounts are set to help the sysop offset the cost of operating the bulletin board. Public bulletin boards are usually run by government agencies, nonprofit organizations, and associations. Both public and private bulletin boards are accessed through local or long distance telephone numbers.

Government bulletin boards post job openings in a special conference area or in a bulletin. BBSs run by search firms usually have an on-line registration process allowing users to enter their qualifications. The search firms then match up the user's qualifications with job requests from employers. Private BBSs contain jobs conferences, classified sections, E-mail areas, and job bulletin board listings. Sometimes, the quickest way to this information is by leaving a message for the sysop on their BBS.

You can locate BBSs in your specific geographic location by contacting a local computer user group. All BBSs have lists of all local and national BBSs available for users. These lists can be downloaded from the BBS computer to your computer via your modem and software. A listing of BBSs across the United States from Darwin Systems, Inc., can be obtained via computer from the Computer Connection at (202) 547-2008.

Resources

The following list of books, commercial on-line services, and BBSs are resources from which you can obtain additional information for using on-line career helpers.

(continues)

Books

*The Complete Book of Personal
  Computer Communications*
Alfred Glossbrenner
St. Martins Press
175 Fifth Ave.
New York, NY 10010
(212) 674-5151; (800) 221-7945
Excellent resource known as the bible
of personal computer communications.
Hands-on tips for working with on-
line utilities, accessing information services; covers topics from telecommuting
to BBSs. 1990.

Commercial On-Line Services

Compuserve Information
  Service, Inc.
5000 Arlington Centre Blvd.
Columbus, OH 43220
(617) 457-8600
Customer Service
  (800) 848-8990
Compuserve is one of the leading on-
line utility services. The "Professional
Forums," a means of exploring job
opportunities, are available for business management, data processing, law-
yers, journalists, and more. Get expert
career tips and advice. Job opening
information is available in *The Association for Education, Journalism and
Mass Communication (AEJMC) Forum,*
and *The Journalism Forum.*

GEnie
GE Information Services,
Dept. 02B
4012 N. Washington St.
Rockville, MD 20850
(301) 340-4000
Customer Service (800) 638-9636
Electronic Registration (Modem)
(800) 638-8369
One-time sign-up registration
charge.
Dr. Job Roundtable is a weekly question and answer column covering career and employment issues. Questions
and comments on career related issues
can be left for Dr. Job and will be
answered privately by E-Mail.

Employment Registries

These are services offered to job seekers allowing them to enter their
work history into a database registry for review by potential employers. Registration can be made on-line or by written application and fees
vary. Check professional and trade associations and other employment
services for computerized résumé services.

Career Doctors
Jeff Altman & Co., Inc.
80 Eighth Ave., Ste. 902
New York, NY 10011
Voice (212) 807-8040
Fax (212) 627-3846
Modem (212) 727-9046
Career Doctors is a bulletin board op-
erated by a professional search firm
specializing in positions in the infor-
mation processing industry. Job listings
include positions in the New York-
New Jersey area and throughout the
United States and Canada. All posi-
tions are fee paid by the client compa-
nies. No registration fee.

Career Placement Registry, Inc.
   (CPR)
302 Swann Ave.
Alexandria, VA 22301
(703) 683-1085

A computerized job-matching service supplying employers and recruiters with résumés of technical and professional job seekers. Applicants enter experience, skills, academic credentials, and career preferences. The database is updated weekly and information remains active for six months. The CPR database is accessible through DIA-LOG Information Services, Inc. DIA-LOG Information (800) 334-2564.

Marlton Career Connections,
   Ltd.
National Data Ctr.
11910-G Parklawn Dr.
Rockville, MD 20852
Registration
Voice (301) 816-9651
Modem (301) 816-9210

Enter your background and credentials into the Professional Registry and your qualifications can be reviewed by thousands of companies. Client companies include Fortune 500 to small firms, private and government institutions, and more. No registration fee.

National JobSearch Network
The Network c/o Employees
   1st, Inc.
P.O. Box 3661
Silver Spring, MD 20901
Voice (301) 593-6775
Modem (301) 681-5331

The National JobSearch Network is "dedicated to providing a forum where prospective employers and job seeking applicants can meet and exchange relevant information." The Network is operated by Employees 1st, a private human resources consulting firm, which provides counseling and other services to employees. There are no charges for using the Network.

SuperResume
Lee Johnson International
The Hearst Bldg., #1125
San Francisco, CA 94103
Voice (415) 788-6000
Modem (415) 546-0119

SuperResume™ is a résumé composition system for experienced Software Engineering professionals. Enter your education, experience, and accomplishments on-line. "*SuperResume* is authorized for use without charge as a publicly accessible, publicly available system for the public benefit."

BBSs

The following are national BBSs that post job opportunities. You can find BBSs that list local and regional job opportunities by contacting local PC user groups. Find these groups by contacting local computer dealers or checking the annual listing of U.S. user groups in:

PC WORLD
501 Second St.
San Francisco, CA 94107
(415) 243-0500

Census Bureau Personnel Division
Modem (301) 763-4574
To speak with a personnel representative (301) 763-5780

Lists Census Bureau vacancies from entry level to senior management.

Federal Library and Information
   Center Network
   (FLICC/FEDLINK) Automated
   Library Information
   Exchange (ALIX)
Modem (202) 707-9656
Voice Phone (202) 707-6454
Lists federal and nonfederal national
library job openings from entry level
to senior level. Provides information
on local BBSs with job openings for
Office of Personnel Management (OPM).

IDI Board
Issue Dynamics Incorporated
901 15th St. NW, Ste. 700
Washington, DC 20005
Lists public interest job opportunities.
Contains a job bank of public and
telecommunications job opportunities
from entry level to senior level.

Office of Personnel Management
   (OPM)
Many regional offices maintain BBSs

for positions in the federal government
in the Office of Personnel Management. Contact your regional office to
find out if they have a BBS.

On-Line Information Access
   Network (OLIAN)
Corporate Information Services,
   Inc.
Box 3880
Reston, VA 22090
Modem (703) 450-1790
OLIAN consists of four different net-
works. The Career Services Network
(CSN) contains company information,
articles, locations, and benefits. The
Career Placement Network (CPN) has
corporate job postings, high tech, and
business. The Investment Network
(TIN) includes personal finances, in-
vesting, and real estate listings. Classi-
fied advertising contains corporate and
private ads. Free limited subscription
for callers providing name, address,
phone number, and company.

Job Banks

Job banks are clearinghouses for job opportunities created by professional and community organizations to assist their members in finding
employment. Organizations often require members to sign a job bank
contract, committing members to pay a small fee for jobs obtained
through the bank.

Job banks operate in a variety of ways. Some list jobs on a phone
line that's updated weekly, while others run lists of jobs in their
newsletters or have members supply postage-paid envelopes that are
used to mail job announcements.

Many of the job announcements include a short description with a
special code. You call another number and once you have verified you
are a member or have a job bank contract on file, you provide the code
and additional information and descriptions follow.

Dial-A-Job

Job lines are appearing all over the country. Many organizations set up
separate phone lines, accessible twenty-four hours a day, seven days a

week, that play a recording of job vacancies. You'll find additional features such as job capsules, benefits information, job closing date, and application procedure. Recordings are updated weekly or bi-weekly.

While the concept is the same, there are many creative names for this service. A recent poll of a Sunday newspaper classified section turned up the following: Dial-A-Job, 24HR Hotline, 24-hour Recorded Jobline, Job Hotline, and Automated Advertising System.

You will most likely find job lines for job vacancies in the federal, state, county, and local governments; hospitals, associations, and non-profits; colleges and universities; and radio and television stations. Employment agencies and companies in private industry have recently joined the bandwagon, so watch for these too. Job line phone numbers are listed by employers in their newspaper classified ads, telephone directories, and organization newsletters.

Local Colleges and Universities

Job announcements are sent to colleges and universities by local and national employers. Each institution has a way of providing this information to their students, alumni, and the general public.

Many organizations display job announcements on bulletin boards or clipboards. Some organizations send out weekly newsletters with job leads to students and alumni. Check with the counseling or placement offices of local colleges and universities to determine how they provide this information.

In-House Opportunities

Every organization uses some type of communication system to announce job vacancies. Many organizations use an internal bulletin board system to post job announcements. Others publish internal opportunities in E-mail and in-house newsletters.

If you are interested in working for a particular organization, do some networking and find out how that organization announces its job vacancies and use your network to keep you informed and updated on job opportunities.

Job Fairs

Job fairs, events where employers set up booths and displays to meet with job seekers, are an opportunity for you to meet employers and explore employment opportunities. You probably won't get hired at a job fair but it's an excellent opportunity for you to make contacts.

Job fairs are organized by colleges/universities, government and community organizations, public and private employment services, associations, chambers of commerce, private employers, and newspapers for the purpose of matching potential employees with potential employers. Fairs can be general, with employers participating from the public and private sectors with a wide range of job openings; specific, sponsored by one industry, such as public education or computers; or for specific positions, such as software technicians.

Employers view the job fair as a recruiting and screening process, gathering qualified applicants for current and future openings. Organizations also use job fairs for public relations, letting you and the community know more about them.

You can meet employment representatives at their booths and gather information about the organization and your career field. There will be company literature ranging from brochures, annual reports, locations, and business cards to benefit descriptions, lists of job openings, general career areas in the organization, and application forms.

Make the most of a job fair by following certain steps. Read the ad announcing the fair and job openings carefully and bring copies of your résumé. Dress professionally and appropriately—the way you envision the individual holding that position would dress. Your personal appearance should reflect the job you are applying for.

Express your interest beginning with the initial contact with the employment representative. Follow all instructions, taking particular care to accurately and thoroughly complete the application. Many people assume that if you have a résumé, you don't need to complete the application. This isn't so. View the application as another opportunity to make a good impression.

Interviews at job fairs are brief and are essentially a screening process. If your interview is favorable, you will make it to the next step, an invitation for a more in-depth interview.

The employment representative at the job fair will give you instructions on the interview process. Depending on how well you do, you may meet with four or five levels during the process.

The interviewer will have a set agenda and you should follow it. Answer the questions asked and be prepared to get in as much information as you can in the little time allotted. You may have just five minutes to sell yourself, so use the time wisely.

Find out when the organization will get back to you and follow up the interview process with a thank-you note. If the organization hasn't gotten back to you by the given time, you can follow up with a phone call and say, "You said you planned on getting back to me within a certain period of time, and I didn't hear yet and wondered where we are." Be very diplomatic in your approach. If you are told that they will get back to you in a week, wait until the week passes before following up again.

The Direct Approach

You may have already identified not only the job that you want, but the organizations that you would like to work for. Or maybe you have narrowed your search based on commuting time, the size of the organization, benefits, or the organization's mission. Whatever the criteria, you can successfully pursue job opportunities yourself. Not only will you be selecting the organizations, but you will be reducing the competition when you apply directly.

Begin your search by researching potential employers from every possible source, from the public library, the employment classified ads and business section of your newspaper, and the local chamber of commerce to your network of contacts.

Plan a strategy for initially contacting these employers by either letter or telephone. Follow up every contact.

Develop effective cover letters directed to individuals in the organizations you've identified. It's easier to manage a job search if you plan on mailing all of your letters at the same time. If you are sending thirty letters, determine when the letters will be ready and have all of the letters dated that day. Mail the letters together, sending an extra one to yourself. You will know the organizations have received their letters when yours has arrived. Allow two to three days for the letter to filter through the organization's mail system before beginning your follow-up calls to arrange job interviews.

Make your phone calls early in the workday or late in the afternoon. Develop a script of what you plan to say and practice it. Plan to make ten calls at once. You'll find you develop a rhythm and gain confidence as you move along. Prioritize your calls, making the most important call last. Keep a log of whom you called, when, the outcome, and further follow-ups. Continue to follow up every lead.

Chapter 9

Interviews That Get Jobs

The job interview is an opportunity for a potential employer to review your skills, abilities, and accomplishments and determine if your qualifications match the requirements for a job opening. And it's an opportunity for you, the candidate, to offer your qualifications as well as ask the potential employer questions about the job and organization to help you decide if you are interested in working in this capacity for this organization.

It sounds simple enough, and yet most job seekers dread and sweat through the interview process.

As Maggie Samuels, recent job hunter, recalls, being prepared isn't always enough:

> I hadn't interviewed in a long time so I made sure that I took the time to carefully prepare for the job interview. I reviewed questions, practiced answers, and contacted my references. One of my references knew the college president personally and was kind enough to write a letter of recommendation to the president's attention.
>
> After all that preparation, the day of the interview finally arrived. I dressed carefully and arrived on time. The secretary escorted me into the dean's office. When I walked into the room, I felt my face get hot and panic spread from my cheeks to my toes.
>
> There were five people waiting to interview me, including the college president.
>
> I found out later, from the dean, that fear was evident in my facial expressions as well as my posture. I had never heard of a group interview before.
>
> It was obvious to everyone that I was nervous. The

president made a joke only I didn't realize at the time that it was a joke and I took offense, which made me even more nervous. He had only been trying to clear the air and relax me. The interview went from bad to worse and after a tense hour, I went home in tears.

A job interview is a time for you to be at your best, so that you can express your strengths and effectively sell yourself. You need to review in an interesting way your past, present, and future; describe what you can bring to an organization, and state why you are the best candidate for the job. If you prepare yourself to be the best, you will be the best.

Types of Interviews

Interviews come in all shapes and sizes and you should prepare yourself to deal with a variety of interview types and situations. Most of us don't like surprises at an interview and you can avoid one if you ask whom you will be meeting with when scheduling your interview appointment.

The most common type of interview is the one-on-one: one interviewer interviewing one job candidate. The interviewer will take either a direct or nondirect approach.

The direct interview is a dialogue of questions and answers: the interviewer asks specific questions about your work experience, career goals, education, training, skills, and community, personal, and leisure activities and you provide the responses. Questions you might be asked are:

"How do you hire?"
"How do you identify system requirements?"
"What experience have you had with financial institutions?"
"What do you see as potentials in this industry?"
"What career goals have you set for yourself?"
"What plans do you have for continuing your education?"
"What skills do you have that will enable you to successfully handle this job?"
"How do you participate in your community?"
"What leisure activities do you pursue?"

If you find you must control questions and answers both, don't panic; you are participating in a nondirect interview. The interviewer may begin with, "Tell me something about yourself," and encourage you with comments such as, "That sounds interesting" or "Can you tell me more about that?" You won't find much direction in this interview situation, and you should be prepared to take the ball and run with it. Use the time to express your qualifications in experience, training, and skills and demonstrate how you can contribute to both the position and organization.

Another type of interview, the defensive or stress interview, places you in a stressful situation while the interviewer assesses your ability to handle pressure. Often in a one-on-one situation, the interviewer may put you in a stressful situation immediately: "I just interviewed six candidates, what makes you think you're any good?" or establish a comfortable rapport then, after you've answered a question, state, "That's the dumbest way to handle that kind of thing." An organization I worked for referred to this tactic as wanting to know if you "could dance," referring not to the tango but to how quick you were on your feet. In other words, how you handled and responded to pressure. The best response to this stressful strategy is to assertively, calmly, and logically answer and explain your accomplishments.

The panel interview brings together two or more interviewers with different perspectives on what they may be looking for in a job candidate. The panel may consist of a representative from personnel to ask general questions, the hiring manager, the person you would directly report to, and someone who is presently in a position similar to the job opening to assess technical knowledge. Questions are likely to be preselected (the process is known as the patterned approach), and all job candidates are asked the same questions. Each panel member rates each candidate after the interview, and when the interview process is completed, the candidates are stack ranked. The candidate with the highest rating is offered the job. Organizations in the public sector favor this approach.

Don't be surprised if you arrive for the interview and find that you are just one of a group of job candidates being interviewed at the same time. While rare, the group interview is often a panel interview as well, offering the interviewers the opportunity to simultaneously assess the interpersonal, communication, and technical skills of several job candidates. The job candidates may all be asked the same question, to be answered separately, or the entire group may be asked a question requiring a group response.

Ten Interview Preparation Tips

1. *Check out the interviewer.* Use your network or research the individual through trade and professional journals.

2. *Contact your references and request permission to use them.* Fill them in on what you are looking for and send them a copy of your

current résumé so they can see what you have been up to. Type your reference's names and phone numbers on an 8 ½-by-11 inch sheet of paper for the interviewer.

3. *Get directions to the location.* Confirm the address, the building, and the floor or suite number. Inquire about parking facilities or accessibility to public transportation. It's always helpful to try a dry run to unfamiliar locations.

4. *Project the image of the positions you are seeking.* Appearance counts. If you are not sure of the dress code, check out the employees at lunch or quitting time. Don't take chances. Inappropriate appearance may cost you the job. Find a professional style that is right for you. The following books will give you visual clout.

The Executive Look
Mortimer Levitt
Atheneum Publishers
866 3rd Ave.
New York, NY 10022
(212) 702-2000
An excellent resource that guides men toward achieving and projecting a professional image. 1985

Looks That Work
Janet Wallach
Penguin Books
375 Hudson St.
New York, NY 10014
(800) 631-3577

Send the right message by creating a professional image that puts your wardrobe and career in harmony. Women only. 1988.

Working Wardrobe
Janet Wallach
Warner Books, Inc.
666 Fifth Ave.
New York, NY 10103
(212) 484-2900, (800) 638-6460
Outlines a capsule strategy for women to look professional without breaking the budget. Wonderful illustrations and easy to follow. 1982.

5. *Thoroughly research the organization prior to the interview using the resources mentioned in Chapter 4.* Write a profile of the organization and develop a few questions based on your research. Place the information in a leather writing portfolio and take it along on the interview.

6. *Familiarize yourself with the types of questions a potential employer can legally ask.* Laws, designed to protect you from discrimination, also prohibit employers from asking questions that violate your civil rights. These laws are in effect for organizations that employ fifteen or more workers. The laws prohibit discrimination on the basis of color, race, sex, religion, national origin, age, pregnancy, childbirth, or related medical conditions. You do not have to answer questions on any of these topics.

7. *Decide what skills, abilities, knowledge, and accomplishments you*

want to relate to the interviewer and rehearse your presentation of them. If the line of questioning doesn't give you the opportunity to speak of these qualifications, take control of the interview. Achieve control by manipulating the answers to questions by adding the information you would like the interviewer to have when making the hiring decision. Carefully list what you have to offer the organization prior to the interview. Reveal details of your personal inventory throughout the interview.

8. *Practice answering questions using a tape recorder.* Prepare a list of interview questions and ask a trusted friend to act as the interviewer and ask the questions. Record the questions and answers and then play back the tape. Is your voice well modulated or shaky and is there any hesitancy? How does your answer sound? Critique your responses and then try again. Continue to work until you hear improvements and feel confident in your voice and responses.

9. *Prepare a closing statement that indicates your interest in the position.* The interviewer lets you know the interview is ending by giving you a nonverbal signal, such as closing a pad, or telling you, "This will be my last question." Now is the time to convey interest. Whether or not you have expressed interest may make a difference in the final selection.

10. *Be on time.* If you are late, your excuse won't matter, whether it was a pile-up on the expressway or no place to park. Plan on getting to the location fifteen minutes early—time to pull yourself together, but not long enough to get nervous.

Fielding the Questions

An interviewer wants to select the candidate who best meets the job requirements. The questions he or she asks will be formulated to determine whether or not you have the necessary qualifications. You need to learn how to express your skills, knowledge, and experience. Provide the interviewer with information that assists him in assessing your credentials.

Types of Questions to Expect

Questions fall into a variety of types. Open-ended questions allow you to answer freely and choose the type of information you want to include in your answer. Hypothetical or situational questions ask how you would handle or what would you do in a work situation.

Don't let interview questions unnerve you. When asked a question, think of what information the interviewer is trying to get from you. It is easier to respond to a question when you understand why the question is being asked.

John Q., recent job hunter, on expecting the unexpected:

> I had been working for the airlines eleven years when a wonderful opportunity opened up. I really wanted the promotion and applied for the job.
>
> I was granted an interview, and the first question I was asked was, "What two words would you like written on your tombstone?" "My tombstone!" I replied, "I'm not dead, I'm here to interview for the promotion!" The interview was awful and I didn't get the job.
>
> I took a class on interview techniques so I would know how to handle myself better for the next opportunity. I learned to identify what information an interviewer is trying to uncover through the questions and realized, too late, that the question about my tombstone was essentially the same as, "What are your strengths?" I did much better at my next opportunity and eventually got a promotion.

Typical Interview Questions

1. What are your strengths? weaknesses?
2. Where do you expect to be in five years?
3. How is your previous experience applicable to the work we do here?
4. Why are you the best candidate for the job?
5. Why do you want to work here?
6. Can you describe for me a typical day in your job?
7. What do you know about our organization?
8. What did you do in your last job to make you more effective?
9. What was the single most noteworthy accomplishment in your last job?
10. What do you look for in a job?
11. Why are you leaving your present position?
12. How long would it take you to make a contribution to our organization?
13. How long would you stay with us?
14. What do you want in your next job that you are not getting now?
15. How would you evaluate your present organization?
16. Why should I hire you?
17. What did you like most about your last job? Least?
18. To date, what have been your two most important career accomplishments?

To Ask or Not to Ask

A successful interview requires participation from you as well as from the interviewer. The more you participate, the more favorable the interview. Always be prepared to ask questions because if you don't you will appear to lack curiosity.

The interviewer preplans questions and so must you. Spend some time prior to the interview jotting down your questions about the job and the organization. Develop questions from the research you've done about the organization. Look at industry trends and opportunities. List your questions on a pad and take the pad with you on the interview. When the interviewer asks you if you have any questions, say yes and open the pad to your list. There is nothing more impressive than an applicant who has taken the time to prepare for an interview.

Questions to Ask

Specific questions about the organization and products or services that you have formulated from your research. For example: "What technical support have you planned for the NASA contract?"

Questions about the competition to show an understanding of the marketplace. For example: "Will you be adding Saturday classes to your curriculum?"

"What position can this lead to?" This shows a desire for growth and advancement and helps you identify whether opportunities here fit in with your career plans.

"What qualities are you seeking for this position?" This gives you the opportunity to relate your experiences, skills, and accomplishments to the job requirements.

If you need to know what the hours are, ask, "What kind of work schedule is expected?"

"Are there periodic performance and salary reviews?"

"What are the organization's plans for expansion?"

"How long has the position been open?"

"What do you expect the employee you hire to accomplish?"

If the interviewer hasn't mentioned salary by the end of the interview, ask, "We haven't discussed salary; can you tell me the salary range?"

Questions Not to Ask

There is certain information that you need to know prior to making an employment decision. But usually, the time to ask these questions is after you have received a job offer. The following questions, although important, shouldn't be asked during a job interview, as they may make the interviewer question your priorities.

"How much vacation, holiday, and sick time will I get?"

"How long is the lunch hour?"

"Are people easy to get along with here?"

"Where will my office be?"

Personal questions about the interviewer, her education and her experience. For example: "Have you ever been laid off?"

Any question that puts the interviewer on the spot. For example: "Does your company permit dating among the employees?"

Questions that imply that you don't know much about the organization and haven't done your homework. For example: "I noticed you are moving to a larger building, so business must be good."

Instead of asking, "What happened to the predecessor?" ask, "How many employees have had this position in the last four years?" "Why are the former employees no longer in the position?" "How many employees have been promoted from this position in the last four years?"

Practice Makes Perfect

The more you know and understand about the interview process, the better you will be. Read all that you can and practice, practice, practice.

Books

The following are highly recommended books.

The Complete Q & A Job Interview Book
Jeffrey G. Allen, J.D., C.P.C.
John Wiley & Sons, Inc.
605 3rd Ave.
New York, NY 10158
(212) 850-6000
Reviews hundreds of interview questions and offers excellent guidelines, ideas, and scripts on how to answer the questions. 1988.

Simon & Schuster Bldg.
Rockefeller Ctr.
1230 Avenue of the Americas
New York, NY 10020
(212) 698-7000
Excellent ideas from résumés to phone tips, timing, interview techniques, references, salaries, and follow-up. This book bolsters your confidence while developing your job-hunting skills. 1983.

How to Turn an Interview Into a Job
Jeffrey G. Allen
Simon & Schuster, Inc.

Interview for Success
Caryl Rae Krannich &
   Ronald L. Krannich
Impact Publications

4580 Sunshine Ct.
Woodbridge, VA 22111-3040
(703) 361-7300
Comprehensive guide to preparing for
interview success. Includes information and resources for the job search
process with particular emphasis on
all aspects of interviewing from networking for the interview, preparing
for the interview, handling questions,
nonverbal behavior, and negotiating
salary. Sample approach, thank-you,
acceptance, and other letters included. 1990.

Knock 'Em Dead
Martin John Yate
Bob Adams, Inc.
840 Summer St.
Boston, MA 02127
(617) 268-9570; (800) USA-JOBS

Worthwhile ideas for answering those
tough interview questions. Provides additional strategies for the search. 1988.

*Sweaty Palms: the Neglected Art
    of Being Interviewed*
H. Anthony Medley
Ten Speed Press
Box 7123
Berkeley, CA 94707
(415) 845-8414
Comprehensive guide providing overall information that will prepare you
and increase your confidence in the
interview process. Easy to read, practical information presented clearly with
follow-up checklists at the end of each
chapter. 1984.

Actions Speak Louder Than Words

Your tone of voice, facial expressions, use of eye contact, and personal
appearance all convey a nonverbal message. Your body language sends
a message to the interviewer, and research tells us that nonverbal
messages carry a far greater impact than the words we speak. If your
verbal and nonverbal messages conflict, the nonverbal will more likely
be accepted and recognized.

Keys to Confident Body Language

1. Enter the room with a straight back and your head held high.
   Use good posture throughout the interview.
2. Forget those weak and limp handshakes. Extend your hand to
   the interviewer and give a firm handshake.
3. Choose a seat close to the interviewer. Position your body
   toward the interviewer and sit straight with your legs planted
   firmly on the floor. Avoid fidgeting. Keep your hands relaxed in
   your lap.
4. Make eye contact throughout the interview. Smile often, when
   appropriate.
5. Modulate your voice and speak clearly. Avoid clearing your
   throat prior to speaking.

The following book teaches how to use body language, silent speech, effectively.

The Secret Language of Success
David Lewis
Carroll & Graf Publishers, Inc.
260 Fifth Ave.
New York, NY 10001
(212) 889-8772
Excellent book with illustrations, examples, and suggestions for exercises to help you make a positive impression on others and sell yourself effectively in interviews. Easy and pleasurable to read. 1989.

It's Not Over Until It's Over

The interview doesn't end when you walk out the door. If you are interested in the job, follow up with a thank-you note, a phone call, or both. Your goal is to make the follow-up a subtle reminder of your interest and qualifications.

Thank-You Notes

A thank-you note is an opportunity to demonstrate courtesy and your ability to communicate in writing. A well-written note could give you a slight advantage, since thank-you notes are not sent that often, and when they are, they are not usually written well.

Begin your note by thanking the interviewer for taking the time to meet with you. Elaborate on your interest and how you can make a contribution. Mail the note within three days of the interview or it will lose its effect.

Phone Calls

It is always appropriate to follow up an interview with a phone call. The purpose of the call is to thank the interviewer for his or her time and reaffirm your interest in the job. The phone call should be short, a reminder and not an intrusion. Never make a pest of yourself.

Job Offers

Congratulations, you've been offered the job! You have handled your search well, but don't lose focus on finalizing the offer and the search in your excitement.

Negotiate Your Salary and Benefits

If you are like most people, you probably find salary negotiations difficult, but it is a skill well worth learning. If you don't do your research and neglect to negotiate the best and most appropriate salary, it will be extremely difficult for you to catch up to others in comparable positions who are being paid more.

Chapter 4 identified resources for researching salaries. You should know what your job is worth in the marketplace and identify what salary you would like and the lowest amount you are willing to take for that job.

Benefit plans now come in all shapes and sizes. Determine what benefits the position offers including health, insurance, retirement contribution, vacation, holidays, training, and tuition reimbursement. Both salary and benefits are often negotiable. If you don't need the health coverage, you can negotiate a higher salary or retirement contribution. Determine your needs and desires prior to negotiation.

Use the tips and strategies in the following resources to become a savvy negotiator.

How to Negotiate a Raise
  or Promotion
Don Weiss
AMACOM Books
135 W. 50th St.
New York, NY 10020-1201
(518) 891-1500
Basic introduction to guidelines on salary negotiations. Effective strategies that really work. 1986.

Rites of Passage at $100,000
John Lucht
Viceroy Press, Inc.
Distributed by Henry Holt and
  Co., Inc.
641 Fifth Ave.

New York, NY 10022
(800) 247-3912
Provides sound advice on negotiating employment packages for individuals in the upper brackets. 1988.

Salary Success
Caryl Rae Krannich &
  Ronald L. Krannich
Impact Publications
4580 Sunshine Ct.
Woodbridge, VA 22192
(703) 361-7300
Good suggestions for identifying what you're worth by conducting your own salary survey, determining salary comparables and the value of jobs, and

dealing with your salary history. Valuable ideas on communicating what you're worth and negotiating salary and benefits. 1990.

The Win-Win Negotiator
Ross Peck & Brian Long
Pocket Books

1230 Ave. of the Americas
New York, NY 10020
(800) 223-2336
Excellent book and philosophy, written in parables that tell how to negotiate favorable agreements that last. Highlights communication skills and how to get along with others. 1987.

The Final Offer

Once you have accepted the job offer, have it confirmed in writing. Ask the employer to confirm the offer by letter and include the salary, salary range, any agreed benefits different from the basic package, starting date, and date of your next performance and salary evaluation. You should receive this letter prior to your first day of work.

Chapter 10

A Never-Ending Process

Have you caught the excitement? You've now got the power and information to create the future you want. The previous chapters identified loads of options for choosing, charting, and directing yourself toward a satisfying career.

It's time to initiate the journey. Remember, you are unique. The options you choose and the plans you make must be at your own pace so they meet your needs. Don't measure yourself against anyone else.

Change produces risk and uncertainty and yet, depending on how you approach it, it can be exhilarating. Planned change is easier to deal with than unexpected change. Risk, though scary by nature, often produces the greatest rewards.

Let's take a look at the options that we've discussed throughout the book and their inherent risks. Each option includes a risk factor. If you combine two options—changing industries and careers, for example—the risk factor increases. But so does the reward. And the results are unmistakably liberating.

Acquiring a New Skill

Risk Factor: **Slight**

Acquiring a new skill enhances your present position and prepares you for future opportunities. Choose a skill that ties in to your present or long-term career goals.

Outline a schedule for acquiring the skill and gaining an expertise. Develop an action plan by choosing a variety of experiences to learn the skill and use every occasion to practice. Incorporate the learning experiences into your daily and weekly routines. **Go to Chapter 5, page 64.**

Seek out others with an expertise in this skill. Solicit their advice on gaining additional experiences. Once you feel comfortable with your skill level, take advantage of every opportunity to practice, polish, and demonstrate your skill.

Enchancing Your Present Position

Risk Factor: **Slight/Moderate**

If you've reached a plateau in your present job, ceased receiving promotions, or just want some change or revitalization without changing jobs, enhancing your present position may be a good option. You can do this by acquiring new work experiences and skills while in your present job.

Some simple activities and involvement on your part can raise your spirits, better your performance, increase your visibility, and prepare you for future moves and changes. Consider contributing articles to a professional journal, developing an internal orientation program, assuming leadership in a professional association, or speaking to local schools about careers in your industry. The possibilities are limited only by your imagination. The following suggestions should spark some ideas.

Join a professional or trade association and become an active participant. Volunteer to chair an activity that will let you enhance or develop a skill—for example, writing and producing a newsletter. Accept leadership roles, and attend programs and workshops. The benefits of participation far outweigh time commitments. **Go to Chapter 6, page 101.**

Expand your network of contacts by setting personal goals for meeting new individuals every week. Give yourself numerical goals so you can measure and reward your results. Opportunities to connect are everywhere; make an effort to get to know individuals in other departments as well as meet people outside your organization. **Go to Chapter 6, page 93.**

Request new work responsibilities. For example, take on a new project, participate in a task force, and lend training support to new employees. Your employer will be pleased with your support and you'll benefit from new or increased work experiences that will expand future options.

Selecting a Different Industry

Risk Factor: **Moderate/High**

If you decide you'd like to change industries, your goal is to become knowledgeable about every aspect of the new industry. You'll need to learn industry terminology and history and about products, services, and companies. Subscribe to industry periodicals and read books about it. Allocate a specific amount of time to do research at your public library. Become knowledgeable about industry potentials and challenges. **Go to Chapter 3, page 35.**

Join a professional or trade association and meet people currently employed in the industry. Demonstrate your experience and skills by volunteering to work on committees. Set a goal to meet employees and decision-makers in this industry. **Go to Chapter 6, page 93.**

If your research reinforces your interest in pursuing employment in this industry, set up informational meetings with hiring managers or individuals currently holding positions you would seek. Continue to build your list of contacts and let everyone know you're interested in changing industries. **Go to Chapter 2, page 29.**

Changing industries does have some risks. You may be able to make a lateral move, but you might have to take a step back to make the transition.

Changing Jobs

Risk Factor: **Moderate/High**

Review the following checklist prior to beginning a job search.

- ☐ Have you kept up with changes in your career field?
- ☐ Are your skills updated?
- ☐ Do you actively participate in professional and trade associations?
- ☐ Do you have professional certification?
- ☐ Do you have the same level of education as others in your field?

You must be able to compete favorably in the workplace and so if you answered no to any of the above questions, it will be worth your time to update your education, skills, and certification prior to beginning a job search.

Assess your skills, accomplishments, experience, contributions, education, and training and write a résumé or job application that highlights your career goals, experiences, and how you can contribute to another organization. You'll use the same type of information to write effective cover letters. **Go to Chapter 7, page 103.**

Identify and add to your network of contacts. Make them aware of your present job search and request their support. **Go to Chapter 6, page 93.**

Develop effective research skills to identify employers you'd like to work for and to learn about particular companies prior to job interviews. If you learn all you can about salaries you'll be in a better position to negotiate the best one for you. **Go to Chapter 4, page 52.**

Use detective skills to uncover job leads. Pursue both traditional and nontraditional sources. **Go to Chapter 8, page 129.**

Sharpen your professional image and interview skills. Job candidates who prepare for the interview are more confident; you'll have greater success if you appear relaxed and self-confident. **Go to Chapter 9, page 146.**

Choosing a New Career

Risk Factor: **High**

Changing careers requires a lot of preparation and entails the greatest risk. Individuals have successfully translated experience and skills into new careers at the same salary and responsibility level, but many career changes wind up taking steps back in salary and responsibility to make the move. You must be prepared to accept less money at first; it will take you some time to regain your salary and responsibility level in the new career. Even if you are ready to accept this, you might encounter problems convincing a potential employer that you are willing to start over again at a lower salary. If you are set on pursuing a new career, don't start from scratch but choose one that builds upon your experiences, skills, abilities, and accomplishments. **Go to Chapter 3, page 35.**

Your first step is determining the educational and experience requirements for the new career area. Once identified, create a list of those you already meet and design a strategy to gradually acquire what's needed. **Go to Chapter 2, page 30.**

If you don't meet the educational requirements, check out flexible college and certificate programs as well as such alternative options as correspondence study. You can fulfill many of the requirements while you're presently employed, making the transition an easier one. **Go to Chapter 5, pages 88 - 90.**

Identify your transferable skills—existing skills that can be used in your new career setting. If you'll need additional skills, devise a strategy to acquire them. **Go to Chapter 2, page 11.**

Check with your employer to see if it's possible to make a career change in your present organization. On-the-job training, shadowing, or tuition reimbursement for outside training or education may be available. You can often make internal changes laterally, reducing the risk factor.

What type of work experiences do you have that relate to the responsibilities in the targeted career? Managing, training, organizing, or administering? Another way to obtain needed experience is to volunteer your time to a nonprofit organization in exchange for the opportunity to gain new experiences.

Apply for and pursue professional licenses and certifications. There are preparation courses and self-study books for most certification exams. **Go to Chapter 5, page 88.**

The quest for satisfying work experiences is a never-ending process. I hope this book has inspired you to think about your whole career and has made you aware of the importance of initiating your own program of change and growth. You can control your career and your future.

Index